CompanyCommand

Unleashing the Power of the Army Profession

NANCY M. DIXON + NATE ALLEN + TONY BURGESS

PETE KILNER + STEVE SCHWEITZER

D1315669

CENTER FOR THE ADVANCEMENT OF LEADER DEVELOPMENT & ORGANIZATIONAL LEARNING

WEST POINT, NEW YORK

Editing: Loren Gary, Lisa Maria Noudehou
Cover Art: Jody Harmon (www.armorart.com)
Illustrator, Chapter 11: Michelle Magnus

ISBN 0-9764541-0-6

Printed in the United States of America

Chris Amos + Eric Atherton + Rob Barnhill + Charles Bowery + Leo Bradley + John Bryan + Kevin Butler + Myles Caggins + Bradford Cary + Maria Chamorro + Jaime Chanez + Sean Cleveland + Traci Cook + George Corbari + Denise Corbari + Angela Crist + Justin Corbett + Lance Curtis + Steve Delvaux + Mark Derber + Dean Dominique + Colin Donlin + Jeb Downing + Fred Dummar + Dan Dwyer + Pete Edmonds + Chris Engen + Paul Evangelista + Sean Farrar + Mark Faria + Dale Fater + Tom Feltey + Sean Fisher + Darren Fitzgerald + Dan French + Gail Gauthier + Chris Gellasch + Joe Grigg + Rob Griggs + Rob Halvorson + Bill Hauschild + Dave Hayhurst + Dan Hibner + Dave Hibner + Jan Holliday + Dan Hubbard + Vickie Hudson + Paul Huszar + Jim Isenhower + Frank Jenio + Charlie Jenks + Claude Johnson + Curt Johnson + Omar Jones + Bart Kemper + Ray Kimball + Seth Knazovich + Matt Konopa +

**We dedicate this book to the CC Team.
Your work *is* making a difference!**

Geoffrey Kuhlmann + Joe Kurz + Cal Kynard + Art La Flamme + Todd Lehenbauer + Vince Lindenmeyer + Brian Locke + Eric Lopez + Christy Lopez + Michael Martel + Patrick McCarthy + Rob McCormick + Will McKannay + Sean McWilliams + Dave Meyer + Patrick Michaelis + Matt Michaelson + John Miller + Jay Miseli + Rob Mitchell + Dan Morgan + Ryan Morgan + Juan Nava + Scott Nelson + Mario Ochoa + Nathan Palisca + Brett Patron + Mike Perkins + Dave Polizzotti + Kristine Quilici + Rich Ramsey + Brian Reed + Michael Richardson + John Ring + Troy Rittenhouse + Luis Rivera + Lynn Rolf + Mike Runey + Steve Ruth + Bobby Sadler + Jeff Sargent + Straus Scantlin + Bradd Schultz + Todd Schmidt + Tim Schnese + Greg Scrivens + Matt Seifert + Scott Shaw + Everett Spain + Cathy Speer + Tim Stiansen + Lon Sunshine + Jordon Swain + Scott Taylor + Darrell Thomsen + Rob Thornton + Mike Titus + Brian Tribus + Mark Tribus + Marshall Tway + Chris Vogel + Greg Wagnon + CP Watkins + Rhett Weddell + Craig Whiteside + John Whyte + Paul Wilcox + Carlos Wiley + John Wishart + Tom Woodie + John Wrann + Dave Wright + Josh Wright + Dave Yebra + Steve Young...

Foreword

by Colonel George B. Forsythe

I first learned about CompanyCommand.com when Nate Allen, one of its founding captains and a former student of mine at West Point, walked into my office with an arm full of butcher paper and asked if I wanted to hear some really cool leader development ideas. (Actually, what he really said was, "Allen of Army reports to the Vice Dean for Education to take his chances," which remains his signature greeting to this day.) Nate had just returned to the faculty at the United States Military Academy to teach leadership. I was eager to hear what he had to say because I had long admired his passion for the study of leadership. Nate spread out on the floor of my office several large pieces of paper full of magic marker diagrams, and he proceeded to describe how a team of experienced company commanders had created a virtual meeting place where company commanders could share with one another what they were learning about company-level leadership. He told the story of swapping ideas with his buddy Tony Burgess on the porch in Hawaii [where they commanded companies in the 25th Infantry Division (Light)] and how wonderful it would be if all company commanders could "meet on the porch." Nate and I talked for over an hour about a wide range of topics—professional connections, knowledge sharing through conversations, individual and organizational learning, leader development, and Army transformation. There on the floor of my office was an innovative and timely vision for the future of the Army, a concept that had the potential to transform our profession from the bottom up. Only after we plumbed the depths of the idea did Nate invite me to view the Web site, which I did with great enthusiasm. It became clear to me that day, as it was to Nate and his teammates, that CompanyCommand.com was not about the Web site. Rather, it was about a community of professionals sharing and learning in a fast-paced dynamic operational context; the technology simply enabled the process. In fact, the more I thought about and observed the CompanyCommand professional forum, the more I realized that the core technology of the forum was the people and the conversations, not the computer.

The growing team of officers who were operating CompanyCommand.com were doing so on their free time, typically in the midnight hours. Given the dramatic response from company-level leaders, this model was not sustainable; they needed support. Our solution was to establish a research and development center at West Point to create space for this idea to fully take shape. Majors Nate Allen, Tony Burgess, Pete Kilner, and Steve Schweitzer lead the new center—the Center for the Advancement of Leader Development and Organizational Learning (CALDOL). Their primary purpose is improving company-level leadership by serving company-level leaders, supporting two professional forums (CompanyCommand and PlatoonLeader), and sharing their lessons learned with the entire Army.

In *Company Command: Unleashing the Power of the Army Profession*, these four majors, along with a leading organizational learning scholar, Dr. Nancy Dixon, serve that purpose by telling the CompanyCommand story. In the book, they speak directly to those who will lead a professional forum; they tell the stories of community members to illustrate the underlying concepts, and they offer practical suggestions for connecting professionals and facilitating conversations.

In reading this book, you will be listening in on a conversation among professionals. You'll see how they share, encourage, support, question, discover, and reason together. To use their words, you will find the stories "awesome, too cool, and amazing." The authors invite the reader to listen and learn; however, they leave much of the interpretation to us, just as they do in the CompanyCommand forum. The book provides a window into the essence of this professional forum—professionals sharing the wisdom of practice and creating new insights about company-level leadership. In so doing, it speaks to a much larger audience than those who would be forum leaders. Anyone who is curious about the structure and dynamics of professional forums will benefit from the stories these authors tell on behalf of the entire company commander community.

Professional forums such as CompanyCommand are at the heart of Army professionalism. As sociologist Dr. Andrew Abbott argues, professions claim jurisdiction for particular work based on abstract expert knowledge. Professional knowledge is more than simply tactics, techniques, and procedures applied to specific circumstances; it is also conceptual understanding brought to bear in unfamiliar situations. The creation, communication, and application of professional knowledge in service of the public good is essential for a profession. Members of the profession have an obligation to acquire, create, and share new knowledge in fulfillment of their commitment to service. *Company Command: Unleashing the Power of the Army Profession* (by the way, this title is no accident) tells the story of how company commanders are fulfilling this professional obligation in new and creative ways. Forums such as this have the power to transform the Army from the bottom up because transformation is as much about human capital and organizational culture as it is about equipment and force structure. The CompanyCommand forum is military professionalism at its best; it is an inspirational example of what the Army profession can be in the Twenty-first Century. Reading this book, I find myself wishing I could go back and do it again, but I take heart in knowing that the Army is in good hands.

A word of caution: be prepared to think about knowledge in new and different ways. Although you will find Standing Operating Procedures, Operations Orders, and Unit Training Plans in the CompanyCommand forum, these objects are not the essential knowledge that community members share with each other. Instead, the knowledge of the community is more dynamic than static; it emerges out of the conversations among participants, is highly contextualized, and changes over time. Much of the knowledge comes from new insights of community members as they participate in the conversations. We in the Army education system are often fond of saying that we want to teach students *how* to think, not *what* to think. That's exactly what is happening with CompanyCommand—the important knowledge of the community emerges from the process of conversation and subsequent discovery, not from the mere posting of specific pieces of discrete knowledge. *How* participants in the forum think about the issues is as important as *what* they discuss. The authors tell us in the introduction that the knowledge of the profession resides in the minds of its members. To take it one step further, community knowledge is also shared knowledge—it resides in the community, not simply in the head of any one individual. This is a novel idea, but one that has powerful implications for leader development, organizational learning, and Army professionalism, implications we are just beginning to understand.

If membership and participation indicate success, CompanyCommand has been enormously successful, and we have much to learn from the authors' experiences. But this book represents a moment in time in what is an ongoing conversation about professional forums and professionalism. Some of what is happening here may apply in other contexts, but I'm sure the authors would challenge new forum leaders to learn by doing. Furthermore, there may be other ways of sharing different types of knowledge; the CompanyCommand model may not necessarily apply everywhere. As the Army evolves as a Twenty-first Century learning organization, we would expect, and indeed encourage, other forms of knowledge sharing.

I'm heartened to think that the Army of the post-Cold War era has nurtured professionals with the commitment, creativity, and vision to build a porch for professional conversation that connects so many fellow professionals. I can only imagine what the Army profession will be like when Soldiers who have grown up with these professional forums are leading the profession in the years to come. I'm inspired and encouraged by the possibilities.

George B. Forsythe
Company Commander
B Company, 2nd Battalion, 6th Infantry
Berlin Brigade, 1972-1974
Vice Dean for Education, USMA

Introduction

"One month ago my company was ambushed in Afghanistan. In fact, we were ambushed on the same road that you will be using as you work in and out of your firebase. Two of my guys were wounded as we fought our way out. We learned some valuable lessons through spilt blood and sweat. I'm here to share these lessons with you so that you can hit the ground running and continue the mission." —Captain Eric Lopez

The cutting-edge knowledge of the Army resides in the minds of leaders at the tip of the spear. Connecting these leaders in conversation brings together the Army's greatest knowledge resources, unleashing the power of the Army profession to improve combat effectiveness.

An illustration of the power of connecting leaders in conversation happened in March 2004, when Eric Lopez and five other officers who had commanded companies in Afghanistan flew to Schofield Barracks, Hawaii, to interact with leaders in the 25th Infantry Division (LIGHT) who were preparing to deploy. For three days these captains shared with Soldiers in the 3rd Brigade Combat Team the hard-earned knowledge they had forged in places like Kandahar, Kabul, and the Shahi-Kot Valley. Their stories about combat operations, the enemy, and the Afghan environment had a directness and immediacy that only someone who had recently led Soldiers in Afghanistan could provide.

Connections and conversations such as these are central aspects of the CompanyCommand "professional forum." The term forum brings to mind the ancient Roman Forum, a gathering place for conversation that served as an incubator for ideas that advanced the entire society. Including the word professional places a forum in the context of a particular profession's advancement, in this case that of the Army. "Professional Forum" thus communicates who participates (members of the profession), why they participate (to improve the profession's effectiveness), and how they participate (with candor and mutual respect). Most of all, it identifies conversation and the exchange of professional knowledge as the defining characteristics.

One way to observe the CompanyCommand (CC) professional forum in action is by logging on to the CC.mil Web site (http://CompanyCommand.army.mil). This Web site enables company commanders to gain access to each other and thereby tap into the collective knowledge of the members. While the Web site may be the visible face of the CompanyCommand professional forum, it represents only one part of the whole. Less visible, but no less powerful, are the many other conversations company commanders are having with each other—by email, on the telephone, gathered around a HMMWV, and in CPs, mess halls, and FOBs around the world.

Such peer-to-peer conversations, in all of their various formats, represent a grassroots movement among company commanders who are discovering that their individual ability to learn and be effective is closely tied to their profession's collective ability to do the same.

The CC Web Site's Beginnings

In the spring of 2000 a team of officers developed and launched www.CompanyCommand.com as a means of connecting past, present, and future company commanders in an ongoing conversation about leading Soldiers and building combat-ready units. Use of the Web site, fueled by word of mouth, spread like wildfire.

The growing team of leaders working to make CompanyCommand.com happen were on a mission to provide cutting-edge, world-class resources for their comrades. They published a book about company command,[1] created a monthly e-newsletter, and began engaging in face-to-face opportunities such as the 10th Mountain Division Pre-Cmd/1SG Course. Along the way, they launched a similar forum for platoon leaders known as PlatoonLeader.org. After two years of continuous growth, the team realized that further development would require organizational support. At this point, senior leaders at the United

---

[1] The book referenced is *Taking the Guidon: Exceptional Leadership at the Company Level*, available via www.TakingtheGuidon.com.

States Military Academy stepped up to the plate and resourced the idea. Without this support, the forums could not have lasted into a third year. In 2002, the CC team officially "gifted" both Web sites to the Army. As a result, the Web sites were placed on military servers at West Point and given ".army.mil" urls,[2] but the vision, the ideas underpinning the work, and the team behind the scenes remain the same.

Four of the authors of this book—Army majors Nate Allen, Tony Burgess, Pete Kilner, and Steve Schweitzer—were part of the team that started CompanyCommand.com. Nancy Dixon, the fifth author, is a knowledge-management researcher and consultant whom the team met in 2002 after reading her book *Common Knowledge*.[3] Nancy interacts with the other four on a regular basis and is an enthusiastic member of the CC team. When the term "we" is used in this book, it refers to these five authors.

The CompanyCommand Professional Forum

One way to describe CC is as a network of company commanders who connect in conversation about relevant content to advance the practice of company command.

- **Connecting** company commanders to each other gives them access to the knowledge of the profession. Having a connection means more than just having contact information—it means being aware of what the other knows. A professional community that is highly connected knows who knows what.
- Connections make **conversations** possible. It is through the back and forth of conversation that context and trust are established and that knowledge is both shared and created. (The reverse, of course, is also true—that is, conversations can create connections that lead to relationships and learning.)
- **Content** grows out of conversations. Content can be both the topic of conversations and an end product. For

---

[2] The original name—CompanyCommand.com ("dot com")—is how many people continue to remember the Web site, and you will see it several times in this book when we directly quote people talking about it.

[3] For more information about Nancy Dixon, visit www.commonknowledge.org.

many of the principles and techniques presented throughout the book.

Part 3

Etienne Wenger, Kent Greenes, and Hubert Saint-Onge—three leading thinkers in the field of knowledge management—share their insights about leading professional forums. Having personally benefited from their mentoring, we are excited to have them share some of their experience and wisdom.

*****

The Army profession is effective only to the degree that its members take responsibility for it, engage in the collective conversation that shapes it, and see themselves as being connected to their fellow warriors—past, present, and future. The profession is like a powerful river—in constant motion as it gains new Soldiers and loses experienced ones—its members learning and innovating as they engage with a rapidly changing environment.

The stories and words of company commanders that are presented here depict a profession that is advancing toward an exciting future. This book is an invitation to members of the Army to connect, to engage with each other, and to unleash the power of the profession.

PART 1

Chapter 1

Connecting Leaders *In* The Experience
To Leaders *With* The Experience

...Three degrees of Stephanie Gray

> Imagine if you will: It is 5 AM and you are "up and at 'em"—you've got a lot to get accomplished today. With coffee in hand, you boot up your computer and scan your long list of unread email. One subject heading jumps out at you: "Assistance with information, Please!" The urgency conveyed in the title catches your attention. You open it and read:
>
> "I'm currently deployed and had a Soldier pass away. I'm looking for funeral detail information on your site and having difficulty. To be exact, I am looking for letters of condolence and other information or memorandums that are needed in this type of situation from a platoon leader, company commander, and S1 perspective. I am currently the S1 trying to do my duties and assist the chain of command in doing theirs through this trying time. It's our unit's first loss and we are all new to this. I would appreciate anything that you can do to assist me."
> —Stephanie Gray
>
> You skim through it, take a deep breath, and read it again. Your day has just changed. You, like any other member of the profession of arms after reading this email, have one thing in mind: to make a difference for Stephanie.

*We dedicate this chapter to Sergeant First Class Ricky Crockett who was killed by an improvised explosive device while he was on patrol in Baghdad on January 12, 2004.

This is the situation that Tony Burgess found himself in on the morning of 13 January 2004. "When I see a request like this one," says Tony, "many things flow through my mind: This is a sensitive topic—not one you want to 'blast to the world'; Who do I know who might be able to help?; What Army resources exist that would be helpful?; Is there any content or are there people with relevant knowledge already available on CC.mil?; How much time do we have?; Who is Stephanie Gray?

"After an initial read of her email, I took a look at Stephanie's dog tag (member profile) and saw that she was a first lieutenant and a Battalion S1. I immediately responded with an email to let her know that the network of professionals she was tapping into would do everything possible to make a difference for her. At the time, the CC team had been gathering input from company commanders with combat experience, to include their insights on dealing with casualties. In my initial response to Stephanie, I included a few of the most relevant comments from the experienced company commanders.

"Until recently, casualty operations had not been a common topic of conversation in the Army. I knew there was not much in the CC online space about it, and I wasn't sure what other Army resources were available. What I did know very clearly, based on our team's past experience, was that there were people out there who had the knowledge Stephanie needed, and we could connect with them. We wanted to help Stephanie while also being conservative in our approach given the sensitive nature of her request. Each situation is unique—it seemed best in this one that we involve as few people as possible while still having the positive impact we desired.

"I sent her request to Pete Kilner and asked him who he knew that could help.[1] I also got in touch with John Miller, an active member of CC who lost a Soldier himself in Afghanistan. During PT that morning, I worked out with Nate Allen—our conversation centered around how we might serve Stephanie. Nate thought of Ray Kimball who commanded in Iraq and who leads the *Soldiers & Families* topic within CompanyCommand—a topic that includes

---

[1] Pete traveled to Iraq during May 2003 and interviewed 80 company-level leaders. A 2nd-order effect of his work was that he was a walking "knowledge map"—perhaps better than anyone else in the Army, he knew who knew what at the company level as far as OIF was concerned.

together and our Soldiers performed extraordinarily under horrible conditions. I knew, in a very personal way, what Stephanie and her unit were going through. So, helping her was very important to me.

"I think this process was pretty basic: One leader had an issue, there was a trusted conduit (CC.com) that connected us, and I shared what I knew. Simple! I probably didn't spend more than 30 minutes on this over the course of a day or two, and I think I made more of a difference in those 30 minutes for the war effort than I have in the months since I got back from Iraq. When you see the direct results of your actions—like with Stephanie—it gives you a real sense of fulfillment."

Stephanie Gray's Reflections

"On my first official day as the S1, our tenth month in Iraq, our unit lost our first Soldier to an IED. The driver of the HMMWV had shrapnel all over the left side of his body, the 1SG (front passenger) had hearing damage, and SFC Crockett received shrapnel to his neck from the back seat. He died prior to getting to the medical facilities.

"I was a pretty junior officer, and I wanted to make sure that I handled the situation correctly. The Command Group was engaged in the immediate issues surrounding the incident and left our firebase to go to the site. I was directed to prepare letters of sympathy and condolence—the initial hope was that SFC Crockett's injuries were not fatal and that the letter of condolence would not be needed. I knew that time would be important. I looked on the CompanyCommand site and couldn't find what I was looking for, so I wrote in asking for help.

"I received replies from several people, some within the hour. I received the rules and regs, pamphlets, letters to use as well as personal advice. *Nothing would have happened in the time frame that it happened without that.* I was able to brief the battalion commander, CSM, and the company commander on everything that we had to do. The people that I was connected to through CompanyCommand gave me everything I needed—I was an expert on the subject matter because of it."

Learning is Driven by Experience

Learning is the process whereby knowledge is created through the transformation of experience. –David Kolb[3]

Where does the current expert knowledge of the profession reside? Primarily in the minds of leaders who are *in the experience* right now. For example, cutting-edge knowledge about commanding in Iraq will be found in the company commanders in Iraq, as well as with those who have recently been through that experience.

Experience is the principal vehicle through which adults learn and develop professional competence. The better they prepare for an experience and the more they make sense of it once they've had it, the more they learn. The following graphic illustrates how individual leaders effectively prepare for and make sense of their experiences, and how leaders who continue the learning process during the experience become even more effective.

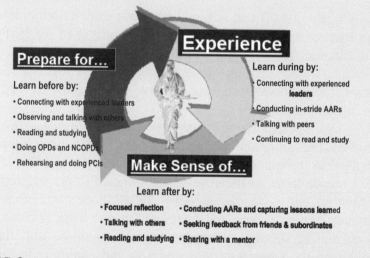

The CC forum supports this learning cycle by serving as a switchboard connecting present, future, and past company commanders in ways that improve their professional competence. By working across the profession, for instance, CC connects leaders who are immersed in a particular experience not only with each other, but also with leaders who have already had that experience. It is also possible to bring future leaders into this conversation—that is, company commanders who are about to have that particular experience. With the needs and demands that arise from a shared experience serving as a crucible, the conversations that CC enables can be transformative.

---

[3] David Kolb, *Experiential Learning: Experience as the Source of Learning and Development*, 1984: p. 38.

Unpacking the Story

A junior officer in a combat zone had a specific question about dealing with a casualty, and she emailed a professional forum coordinator asking for help. In return, she was connected with officers who had relevant and recent operational experience dealing with casualties—experts who brought their collective wisdom to bear for her, allowing her to act in the moment with competence informed by experience.

Connecting people

You have probably heard it said that we are connected to any person within six degrees.[4]   In this story, CC served as a gateway—giving Stephanie access to the knowledge of the profession within three degrees: Tony to Pete to Will; Tony to John to LTC G; Tony to Nate to Ray. This story bears out the assumption that in a tightly connected community like CC, members are no more than three degrees of separation from people whose experience and perspective can improve their effectiveness immeasurably.

Since we believe that the knowledge of the profession resides primarily in the minds of its members (see the "Learning is Driven By Experience" sidebar), we place great value on people-to-people connections. Granted, a professional forum has to have good content that is readily available to its members. But, although she may not have realized it when she first asked for help, Stephanie needed more than factual information about casualty operations. By connecting her with people who had been through experiences similar to hers, CC enabled Stephanie to learn far more than if she had simply been given access to a repository of content.

LTC G's response to Stephanie illustrates this point. He attached content (a copy of a letter of condolence he sent to a Soldier's family), and he placed it in context by describing the kinds of things he would be doing if he were in her shoes. He gave

---

[4] In his 1967 paper, "The Small World Problem," Stanley Milgram argued that everyone is separated from everyone else by approximately six degrees—in other words, you can connect anyone to anyone else in the world through a chain of no more than six people. Most people know this concept through the game "Six Degrees of Kevin Bacon." The idea is to link actors to Kevin Bacon through the movies they've been in, using no more than six movies.

Stephanie contextual understanding and tacit know-how about how to craft the letter—something Stephanie would not have benefited from without the person-to-person connection.

There are two crucial factors influencing whether a connector can successfully bring together the person who *needs to know* with people who *know*. First, a connector must become aware of a specific need (e.g., Stephanie's request). Second, a connector must know who has relevant experience and knowledge (e.g., John Miller, William Glaser, Ray Kimball).

Finally, by connecting with people, conversation can occur. A request can be clarified. A second question can be asked. Context and trust can emerge that allows additional value to flow. For example, Stephanie wrote William back asking additional questions. As a result of the ongoing connection and conversation with Stephanie, William tapped into his old battalion and brigade chaplains to get the specific answers she needed. Simply stated, connecting people allows the knowledge of the profession to flow from those who *know* to those who *need to know*, from those with specific experience to those who need that experience right now.

Professional community

As members of the Army profession, we are part of something larger than ourselves. We share common values, a commitment to being competent—both individually and as a group—and a desire to give back and to make a difference for fellow professionals. This sense of professional identity helps set the conditions that make a forum like CC possible. Additionally, CC is always looking for opportunities to strengthen this sense of professional identity. In the Stephanie story, this theme of professional community occurs in three distinct phases: before, during, and after.

Before Stephanie's request. When Stephanie was a second lieutenant based out of Fort Bragg, North Carolina, she was placed in command of her signal company when the company commander was deployed to Afghanistan. On the advice of her mentor, she tapped into CompanyCommand.com. What she found there was invaluable. Stephanie writes:

> I used CompanyCommand to help with my command philosophy, planning and executing my "commander's week," training meetings, counseling, my OER support form, different issues that used to come up with Soldiers, and a lot of other stuff. I am not sure how I would have been so successful as an acting commander being new to the Army and the unit. CC.com became my best friend.

CC had become part of the way Stephanie learned. And long before she wrote in with her question from Iraq, CC had earned her trust.

In addition, CC had been working all along to create high-trust relationships among its members. Because those relationships—for example between Tony and John, Nate and Ray, and Pete and Will—were already in place, the informal network was able to respond quickly and effectively when Stephanie's call for help came. A critically important point here is that connectors must not only know who knows what, they must also have a trusting relationship if they hope to inspire participation. The relationship between Pete Kilner and Will Glaser makes this point. Although they weren't "friends," Pete connected with Will face-to-face in Iraq. Pete interviewed him there and established a connection, a bond with him. Moreover, Pete had published Will's story in the Warfighting section of CC.mil. Thus, Pete writing him and asking him to help Stephanie was different than if he had never met him and had no relationship or level of trust established. The power of this relationship/trust factor cannot be overestimated.

During the process of responding to Stephanie's request. From the standpoint of fostering professional camaraderie within the forum, a request for assistance is a critical event. CC team members responded to Stephanie with the clear understanding that the interaction would shape her impression of CC in the future; they saw the request as an opportunity to deepen her relationship with the forum. Moreover, experiences like this one also have a positive impact on members like John and Will who take the time to share their experience in such a meaningful way.

Reinforcing a sense of professional community during this experience was the tone of the emails sent to Stephanie: professional to professional, one comrade to another. LTC G's correspondence with Stephanie is an excellent example of this tone. Despite the difference in rank, his email was written in the spirit of one warrior writing to another.

After Stephanie's request. Several days after his initial contact with Stephanie, Ray followed up with her to see if she needed anything else. He also sent her a CC "dog tag" coin to thank her for initiating a series of interactions that led to new content being created for CC.mil that would benefit other leaders down the road.

Tony and Nate followed up with the CC members who had taken the time to help Stephanie, making sure they understood how their contributions had benefited Stephanie and her unit. A few minutes devoted to saying thank you and to giving specific feedback about the impact of the contribution recognizes the effort taken, reinforces a sense of meaningful contribution, and hopefully encourages further participation in the forum.

We have found that relationships, trust, and a sense of professional community are critical factors that set the conditions for interactions like the one with Stephanie to occur. These factors can be overlooked or underappreciated because they are intangibles and so often invisible without an intentional awareness. Every positive interaction is a reinforcing process that creates stronger relationships, more trust, and a greater sense of professional community.

Content

To be effective, a professional forum must continually create new content to meet members' evolving needs. In the experience of helping Stephanie, Ray Kimball realized that there was a content gap in the *Soldiers & Families* topic. That recognition, combined with the fact that casualty operations would be a growing concern for company commanders, caused Ray to respond. He created a topic specifically for casualty operations immediately—in fact, he sent the link to Stephanie within days of her initial note, in time for her to make use of it. Ray has since continued to pull in content and people's experiences, and has sparked conversation about the topic in a way that will be of value to future Stephanie Grays.

The Stephanie Gray story shows that the Army's greatest asset is the experience of its members. The more we connect people, spark conversations, create content, and foster a sense of professional community—the more effective we will become.

Key Concepts—Chapter 1

- The knowledge of the Army profession resides primarily in the minds of its members.

- Connecting members allows the knowledge of the profession to flow from those who *know* to those who *need to know*, from those with specific experience to those who need that experience right now.

- Who professional forum coordinators know and the quality of their relationships with members of the community determines their ability to serve members.

- Person-to-person connections and conversation allow context and trust to emerge and additional knowledge to flow.

- Relationships, trust, and a sense of professional community are critical factors that set the conditions for effective connections and conversations. Moreover, each positive interaction is a reinforcing process that creates stronger relationships, more trust, and a greater sense of professional community.

- Content development is a dynamic interplay between emerging needs and professional forum leader awareness and initiative.

- A tightly connected, decentralized network of leaders can quickly link members to knowledge and resources that might otherwise be inaccessible.

Chapter 2

The Hubbard Effect

…The power of face-to-face connections

> 26 August 2003. Captain Dan Hubbard's 3rd Infantry Division armor company just redeployed from SW Asia. His unit had engaged in fierce combat in the "Thunder Run" attack into Baghdad and had then conducted security operations in Fallujah. Put yourself in his shoes. Your unit is in the throes of refit and recovery on a major scale and you, along with every Soldier and family in the outfit, are eagerly awaiting the block leave that is now just days away.
>
> Then, you get a call from Pete Kilner, whom you met on the ground in Iraq when he interviewed you about your combat-leadership experience. Pete excitedly asks you to travel with him and several other members of the CC team to Germany where they will be leading small-group workshops over several days with company-level leaders who are preparing to deploy to Iraq (OIF 2). Pete makes a strong case for the impact that you will have on the leaders as they train their units for combat in the very place you just left.
>
> *Will you go to Germany for a week?*
> *Or, will you take all your well-earned block leave?*

The workshops that the CC team invited Dan to participate in were to be conducted at the US Army Europe Land Combat Expo and, as you might have guessed, Dan agreed to join the effort, flying to Germany just two weeks after the initial invitation. His involvement proved to be instrumental in the success of the workshops, so much so that we began calling the type of impact he had the "Hubbard Effect."

The *Hubbard Effect:* The powerful learning that results when we tap first hand into the experiences of those who have recently done what we are preparing to do.

The CC team is constantly looking for opportunities to add value to company commanders, and therefore jumped on the opportunity to lead workshops at the Land Combat Expo—especially knowing that most of the participants were preparing for Iraq. Whereas the Stephanie story demonstrates what is possible when it comes to online connections, this chapter underscores the impact of face-to-face connections.

Nate Allen helped coordinate the team's efforts at the Land Combat Expo: "We wanted participants to leave each workshop equipped with ideas and insights that would directly impact their effectiveness in combat," Nate recalls. "As we described in Chapter One, Pete Kilner deployed during OIF 1 to Iraq where he interviewed over 80 company-level leaders. Although he had relevant and hard-hitting insights that would clearly add value, we felt that there was something missing. With only two weeks to go, the idea emerged to have a current company commander—one with experience commanding in Iraq—come with us in order to share from his or her first-hand experience. Pete thought of Captain Dan Hubbard who readily agreed and sacrificed time with family in order to join us.[1]

"We arrived on the ground in Germany two days before the first workshop intentionally to prepare. As we rehearsed, we realized that to make the lessons Dan and Pete had learned in Iraq really come alive, they would need to share them as stories.

"We counted 70 leaders sitting around the tables as we started the first workshop. Following our plan, the first of three parts of the workshop consisted of small group discussions about leading and building a winning team. We presented some initial ideas and then asked the participants to discuss them with the other leaders at their table, relying on their own knowledge to create relevant and engaged discussions. They discovered, as we expected they would, that there was an enormous amount of competence and expertise sitting to their right and left.

---

[1] Although this sounds simple in retrospect, at the time we weren't sure if we could find a CO who was back from Iraq and able to fly to Germany on such short notice.

"The second part of the workshop focused on preparing a winning team for combat—combat in Iraq. Dan shared his stories from a very tactical perspective. For example, he told a story about getting on the radio just before LD, cracking a joke, and then setting a tone across his unit for a resolute and calm advance forward. Pete subsequently provided a broader understanding of challenges across the entire region based on the many interviews he had conducted in Iraq.

"Pete and Dan went back and forth, each talking to the same key learning point. Dan would share a personal experience and Pete would follow with a couple of vignettes that reinforced that same point in a different context. These stories became the vehicle through which lessons such as 'You will fight as you trained' and 'Stay calm on the net' were made 'sticky' or, in other words, 'lodged in the brain' in such a way that the lessons stayed with the participants and influenced their future behavior in combat.

"The final part of the workshop consisted of small group discussions that we drove with this question: 'So what? What are you going to do as a result of what you've heard today—how will this impact how you prepare your team for combat?' These final discussions actually turned out to be the most exciting. We could sense the energy and buzz in the room as these leaders got into conversations about things that they were passionate about.

"After that first workshop, Dan was mobbed as leaders gathered around to ask specific questions and to thank him. When we finally walked out of the room together—long after the workshop had formally ended—Dan quietly said, 'I'm not sure who got more out of that, them or me.'"

Dan Hubbard's Reflections

"The opportunity to make a difference for so many fellow professionals is the most memorable part of the experience for me. At the time, Iraq was just developing and I could tell that what I shared would have a direct impact on how the attendees would prepare their Soldiers for combat. My personal highlight was participating in the table discussions toward the end of the workshop. These conversations didn't stop there, though. I was bombarded after the Land Combat Expo, receiving over 70 emails asking for specific TTPs and advice. Some notes contained numerous questions and others were one liners. Many of the questions seemed to be driven by specific issues that came up during unit training. As I read some of them, I could picture an NCO asking their commander a question like, 'Hey, sir, how are we going to conduct this patrol while operating a tactical check point?' And the CO being able to say, 'Let me talk to a friend, and I'll get back to you.' Well, I was that friend. Let me tell you, I had to go back and put my thinking cap on with some of the questions sent my way. I wouldn't trade this professional exchange for the world!

"I made many new friends through this experience, and I have continued to stay in contact with some of them while they are deployed in Iraq. Captain Bolke is an example of one of these leaders. He was getting ready to take command, and so his first questions revolved around establishing himself as a commander and creating a positive climate in a unit preparing to deploy. His questions shifted toward specific tactical types of issues and combat leadership as his unit hit the ground in Iraq. What's exciting is that the dialogue has helped me out a ton also. I'm currently a unit trainer for the 278th ACR, Tennessee National Guard. Captain Bolke has kept me current and relevant by sending me updates on evolving TTPs. I've been able to pass these on to the 278th ACR as I help prepare them for their deployment to Iraq.

"Secondly, I personally developed in a big way as a result of the experience. This was the first time, besides being with my company, that I'd been up front sharing with other leaders what I had learned in combat. I would say that as a result of taking the opportunity to share in this manner, I'm at a whole different level in my own thinking and ability to communicate with others. The process of reflecting on my experience, unearthing lessons, and then crafting a story that brings those lessons to life is hard work! The Land Combat Expo has been a building block for me in what I'm doing now. I'm constantly asked to conduct OPDs and I model every one of them after the way we executed at the Land Combat Expo. I envision continuing to create these types of professional conversations in the future no matter what job I'm in.

"This was one of the most professionally rewarding experiences I've ever had. I honestly didn't think beforehand that it would make this kind of difference, but as people were coming up to interact with me, I felt I truly had a purpose for being there."

Kenneth M. Koyle's Reflections

"As a workshop participant, Captain Hubbard's presentation had a deep impact on me and my company. He told a story about 'crossing the berm' with his armor company and making a company net call over the radio to get his Soldiers to relax and build their confidence in the mission they were undertaking. When my convoy of 40 vehicles and 88 personnel crossed that same berm on the way to Tikrit in March 2004, tensions were high. Although our situation was different—we were a convoy of wheeled vehicles on an approach march to an established FOB instead of an armor company on the initial attack—my Soldiers were extremely concerned about IEDs, ambushes, and the known threat. Where Captain Hubbard's company faced a largely unknown threat, we knew what was going on to the north—convoys getting blown up and Soldiers dying every day. A lot of Soldiers feared the worst. But as we crossed into Iraq, I remembered what Captain Hubbard had said about the radio call and the effect it had on his men. I did the same thing: I got on the radio, welcomed my Soldiers to Iraq, and gave them a very short pep talk. About 30 miles into Iraq, we had a vehicle breakdown and had to conduct the first of several maintenance halts on the highway. At the halt, I moved from Soldier to Soldier, expressing my confidence in them and telling them what a great job they were doing. It all helped, and many of the ideas I put into action as I entered Iraq were ideas born in the conversations with Captain Hubbard at the Land Combat Expo."

Unpacking the Story

The Stephanie story is an example of a leader in the *middle* of an experience tapping into the knowledge of experienced members of the profession. In this chapter, a group of leaders *preparing for* a specific experience meet face-to-face in a workshop with an experienced leader. Several factors at work in this example—relevant content, context, and conversations—came together to produce the *Hubbard Effect.*

Relevant content

Dan's experience, communicated through the power of stories, was the content of the workshops and drove the conversations and learning that occurred. Stories that communicate important lessons are dramatically more effective than *PowerPoint* bullets, and the use of stories is a critical part of creating the *Hubbard Effect*. However, the process of crafting a story based on personal experience takes time and requires practice. Dan rehearsed his stories several times and delivered them in an authentic, humble way. Because Dan told stories about his actual experience, the main content of the workshops was Dan himself—the messenger in this case was the message.

"What makes content relevant?" Or, as in this case, "What makes the experiences of a person like Dan Hubbard relevant?" To some extent, it was his personal presence and the power of his stories. However, there are two additional factors that seem to influence how relevant a person's experience is:

1. **How timely is the experience?** A current company commander values the experience of a leader who commanded a company ten years ago, but perceives the experience of a leader who commanded six months ago as more relevant. This distinction is especially true in today's rapidly changing environment. Dan's experience was as timely as you could possibly get since he had just redeployed from Iraq.

2. **How comparable is the experience?** Leaders value the experience of another person in direct proportion to how comparable the other person's experience is to the one they are preparing for. If you are a company commander preparing for combat operations in Iraq, you place more value on the company commander with experience in Iraq than the commander with experience in Kosovo; similarly, the experience of an HHC Commander in Iraq is more relevant to other HHC Commanders than the experience of a line commander. The fact that Dan had come directly out of Iraq and that the participants were deploying to Iraq made his experience exceedingly relevant.

In Praise of Workbooks

In the Land Combat Expo, we created a workbook that provided space for participants to make notes. This format allowed them to create their own content that they could return to in the future. In addition to giving them structured space to take notes, we included content from the CC online space like excerpts from the interviews Pete did in Iraq, including the one with Dan Hubbard. This was relevant content; it also introduced the participants to another resource that was available to them.

Context

At the Land Combat Expo, we worked to shape context on two different levels. The first was the level of the participants themselves. Since they were primarily company-level leaders on notice for deployment, we built our plan with a focus on the domain of company-level leadership and preparation for combat in Iraq. While this approach sounds obvious, its importance cannot be overstated. Understanding the participants' context up front is what ensured that the content we created for the workshop was relevant content, and it is what led to Dan Hubbard's involvement.

The second level of context had to do with the lessons that Dan and Pete shared. These lessons were not new: we have all heard "stay calm on the net" many times. But through their stories and vignettes, Dan and Pete were able to place those familiar lessons into rich and detailed context that greatly increased their relevance and made them sticky. Elements such as the situation in which a lesson was learned, the outcome, the time-frame, and who was involved all add to an understanding of the lesson's context. This type of contextual knowledge is inseparable from content. In fact, we would go so far as to say that **content without context is empty and powerless to affect learning**. We want every piece of content and every lesson we share to be enriched with the context in which that lesson was developed and learned.

One leader's effective technique applied without thought by another leader may not produce the same positive outcome—what works for a leader on the ground in Kosovo may not be effective in Iraq. But placing the technique in context helps reveal its underlying principles, which enables the leader to modify the lesson for a different situation. This context allowed Ken Koyle to appropriately apply Dan's lesson, "Stay calm on the net," as he crossed the berm with his own company into Iraq six months later. Context allows a lesson to become a lesson learned.

Conversation

Relevant content, in context, creates the conditions for powerful learning to occur. However, it is through conversations that the fruit of the *Hubbard Effect*—learning and increased effectiveness—is realized. This was especially evident at the Land Combat Expo. It was in the small group discussions that leaders were able to ask questions, challenge assumptions, and take ownership of the workshop.

Throughout each workshop, we paused and asked participants to engage with each other about what they were learning or about an experience they themselves had that was relevant to the topic being covered. This focus shifted the role of our team from that of *expert* to that of *facilitator, participant,* and *co-learner.* Dan, for example, used his stories to generate conversations at the round tables rather than as a vehicle just to dispense his knowledge. Knowing that it is in these conversations that the real learning occurs, we consistently cut the amount of content we cover in order to create space for meaningful conversations among the participants.

We consider encounters with leaders like the workshop participants to be part of an unfolding relationship. For some participants, it was a deepening of an already existing relationship, and for others, it was a beginning. When the workshops in Germany ended, the conversations really began. Participants used the workshop experience as a catalyst for conversations in their units. Moreover, one third of the participants continued the conversation by emailing Dan specific questions even after they deployed to Iraq! This "conversation beyond the event" is an essential part of the *Hubbard Effect.*

Finally, it's important to make note of Dan's learning. We often emphasize members helping or giving back to others; however, the person who "gives back" benefits greatly as well. After the first workshop, Dan said to Nate, "I'm not sure who got more out of that, them or me." Dan is now a more effective teacher, and he tells us that he's able to stay current and train his own Soldiers better as a result of relationships he developed with several of the workshop participants.

*****

The principles that we have discussed in this chapter apply equally to face-to-face and online communication. Whenever we engage with members, we seek to bring to bear content that is relevant and situated in rich context. Furthermore, we use that content as a catalyst for conversation.

Key Concepts—Chapter 2

- Content relevance increases as timeliness and comparability of experience increase.

- Conversations unleash learning and create shared meaning.

- The leaders of a professional forum must see themselves as facilitators, participants, and chief learners—not as experts or dispensers of knowledge, especially in a constantly changing and uncertain environment.

- The value of face-to-face communication increases when you identify what members in your community are preparing for, connect these members with leaders who have relevant experience, and create the space for conversations to occur.

Chapter 3

Talking About Books

...How commanders are using professional reading to "target the learning curve"

As the Stephanie Gray story and the *Hubbard Effect* demonstrate, online connections and face-to-face gatherings are powerful means of creating conversations that impact leader effectiveness. A growing number of leaders are also using professional reading as a catalyst for conversations within their units—shifting the emphasis from the reading to the conversation about the reading.[1]

To support and encourage this type of professional reading, the CC team has created the *Pro-Reading Challenge*. We provide company commanders with copies of a book of their choosing and create a space online for them to discuss it. "When you and your leaders read together with an eye toward practical applications," we tell company commanders, "the conversations that result will improve your unit's performance." The specific type of reading—whether a book, a chapter in a book, a journal article, or perhaps content from CompanyCommand.army.mil—is not what's most important about the challenge. The emphasis of the challenge is on the conversations *about* the reading, which happen when the leader creates space for it—during a meal, around the HMMWV hood, or even online. The very first unit to take the challenge was HHC/1-509th (ABN), part of the JRTC OPFOR Battalion at Fort Polk, LA.

---

[1] Army leaders have long regarded professional reading as an important part of their personal development, and there is a time-honored tradition of encouraging one's subordinate leaders to read. The typical model, however, focuses on the individual—reading is something you do on your own, and what you learn depends on what you alone get out of it.

They selected *Leadership, The Warrior's Art,* a great book coauthored and edited by Chris Kolenda. The participants—the specialty platoon leaders, primarily—read the book and captured what they were learning in an online forum set up for them within CC. This first experience was especially memorable: not only did Chris Kolenda personalize each book with a note and his signature, he also joined the online discussion.

Although very few "outsiders" (people who weren't part of the HHC/1-509th) posted comments, it became apparent to us that the wider profession was listening in on the conversation—among them, leaders throughout the battalion (1-509th). Ron Clark, the battalion S3 at the time, told us that the battalion staff officers were discussing with each other the insights that the lieutenants involved were making online. The battalion commander commented to Ron that he was really impressed by the depth of the lieutenants' understanding about leadership, especially that of one platoon leader who was typically very quiet.

Another example of the wider profession benefiting from this one reading program was revealed in an email sent to us by a company commander stationed hundreds of miles from Fort Polk:

> CC.com has been a beacon of light for so many officers. I make it almost mandatory for my leaders. As a result, instead of "Good morning, sir!" I am approached by my lieutenants with, "Did you see the discussion on *The Warrior's Art* yesterday?" on more than one occasion.
> —Chris Amos, 2101st TC (ALARNG)

In this way, one company's reading program can become a learning event for leaders across the Army.

We emerged from this first reading-program experience thinking, "This will work!" The program, under the leadership of Steve Delvaux and then later Mike Runey, has taken on different forms, but has consistently served as a catalyst for professional reading, conversation, and learning about warfighting and leadership. In 2004 alone, more than 35 units took the *Pro-Reading Challenge.* Below, we share the experiences of two units, illustrating the variety of strategies and the depth of impact possible with this program.

Todd Schmidt Takes the *Pro-Reading Challenge*

Unit: A/1-62 ADA, 25th Infantry Division (LIGHT), Schofield Barracks, Hawaii
Book Choice: *Taliban*, by Ahmed Rashid
Context: Preparing for Combat Operations in Afghanistan

"As we prepared for deployment to Afghanistan, my 1SG and I wanted to ensure that our leaders and Soldiers were grounded in basic knowledge about Afghanistan to include Islam, the culture, the history, and the language," writes Todd from Afghanistan. "We partnered with CC's *Pro-Reading Program*, and chose Ahmed Rashid's book, *Taliban*. Mike Runey and team sent us free copies of the book and opened up a discussion forum for us in the professional reading section of the Web site. I sparked the online conversation with questions to focus my leaders in on some key aspects of the book, and we were off to the races.

"We also tied the online discussion to a series of OPDs we were doing as we prepared to deploy, which included simple face-to-face discussions as well as special events. For example, we invited a leading scholar on Islamic culture to speak to our leaders and to answer questions. He was born and raised in the Kandahar region and gave us an extremely credible sense of Afghanistan's history and the key events we needed to know about.

"We also asked the president of the Muslim Association in Hawaii to speak to our Soldiers. He did a fantastic job of educating us about cultural issues including things to say/not to say, appropriate gestures, and appropriate interaction with women. Afterward, we had an authentic Afghani meal, complete with ethnic music and burning incense. Our intent was for the key leaders in the battery to hear, smell, taste, and touch a small part of where we were going. These experiences and the book we were reading were mutually reinforcing, each giving the other context and greater meaning.

"One interesting thing about the online discussion was that it caused people to think deeper about what they were learning. Instead of skimming the book or listening to the speaker and then forgetting about it, we were writing down what we were learning. And because we were reading each other's comments, the team became aware of what others were learning. It's cool when you write down what you got out of a chapter and then read what the other leaders got out of it. Given how busy we were, this combination of face-to-face experiences and conversation, coupled with the online reflection, turned out to be really valuable.

"Now that we are here on the ground in Afghanistan, I'm finding that the study we did of the people and culture is paying huge dividends. One insight that we gained from reading and discussing the book was that *aspects* of the Taliban movement in Afghanistan were positive. That topic of conversation laid the groundwork for us to more effectively understand a key part of our policy over here: helping disaffected Taliban rejoin a legitimate governing process. In the words of our allies over here, 'Not all Taliban are terrorists, and not all terrorists are Taliban.'

"A second example is the Afghani tendency to switch alliances out of convenience. Our natural reaction is to judge that kind of behavior as unprincipled and disloyal. The discussions we had after reading *Taliban* allowed us to see the bigger picture when we got here to Afghanistan. When we did a two-week operation in the Zabol Province and the Arghandab Valley, for example, where no coalition forces had ever been, the people actually thought we were Russians! When they figured out who we were, they were extremely supportive. Two weeks later, after coalition forces departed the area, the enemy (ACM) came right back in and filled the void. Until there is enduring security and freedom in Afghanistan, it should not be surprising that the people appear to switch loyalties—they have been doing it for hundreds of years in order to survive.

"In closing, I'd say that reading a book is not a silver bullet. It was valuable to us because it was integrated into supplemental OPDs that brought it to life, as well as face-to-face and online discussions. All that, together with our combat training, prepared us immensely for the mission we are currently conducting. As a result, we hit the ground running with much greater understanding and judgment about issues."

Targeting the Learning Curve

The learning curve depicts the relationship between effectiveness and time in a particular experience (see diagram below). For example, it is to be expected that a company commander's effectiveness will increase the longer she is in command. This process of development is illustrated below as movement up and to the right along the learning curve.

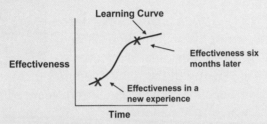

Moving along the learning curve is certainly desirable, but leaders are primarily interested in shifting their learning curve up and to the left. In this way, company commanders will go into each experience they have at a higher level of effectiveness, potentially saving months of on-the-job learning. In addition to being more effective from the outset, leaders will be able to learn more from the experiences that they have.

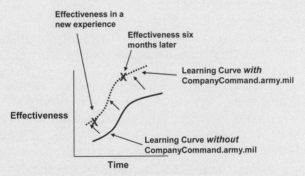

Todd Schmidt applied this thinking to his leader team as they prepared for combat operations in Afghanistan. Using the book *Taliban* along with an amazing professional development program, he was able to create a new learning curve for his leaders. As a result, they arrived in Afghanistan at a higher level of effectiveness. Moreover, Todd's leaders will likely continue to learn at a higher rate throughout the experience as a result.

Scott Shaw Takes the *Pro-Reading Challenge*

Unit: A/2-14 IN, 10th Mountain Division, Fort Drum, NY
Book Choice: *The Killing Zone: My Life in the Vietnam War*, by Frederick Downs
Context: Immediately prior to a deployment to Iraq

"I selected *The Killing Zone* for three reasons," writes Scott Shaw from Iraq. "First, it is the story of an infantry platoon leader in Vietnam who faced many of the same dilemmas that junior officers are facing today. Second, I read it and was influenced by this book myself when I was a rifle platoon leader. And third, the platoon leader in the book was a member of our regiment; this gave us a link to the past.

"In our online space, I posted the following intent:

> ### The Commander's Intent
>
> 1. Examine how a fellow PL thinks through things in a combat zone. In specific, how a platoon leader controls his AO.
> 2. Better understand the PL/PSG relationship. I think that this book shows a couple pretty good examples.
> 3. Evaluate how platoons move within a company zone. We haven't done it for a while.
> 4. Assess a true LIC environment and how what the "big Army" sees as LIC, the squad leader and rifleman see as high-intensity conflict.
> *Click to find out more about the book.*

"Since a book is too much to study at one time, I divided the book into four reading sessions based on the sections of the book. Mike Runey—the *Pro-Reading* coordinator—and I developed four questions to drive the online conversation, and posted them over the course of three weeks:

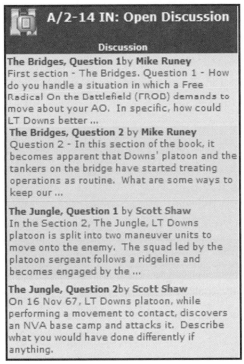

A/2-14 IN: Open Discussion

Discussion

The Bridges, Question 1 by **Mike Runey**
First section - The Bridges. Question 1 - How do you handle a situation in which a Free Radical On the Battlefield (FROB) demands to move about your AO. In specific, how could LT Downs better ...

The Bridges, Question 2 by **Mike Runey**
Question 2 - In this section of the book, it becomes apparent that Downs' platoon and the tankers on the bridge have started treating operations as routine. What are some ways to keep our ...

The Jungle, Question 1 by **Scott Shaw**
In the Section 2, The Jungle, LT Downs platoon is split into two maneuver units to move onto the enemy. The squad led by the platoon sergeant follows a ridgeline and becomes engaged by the ...

The Jungle, Question 2 by **Scott Shaw**
On 16 Nov 67, LT Downs platoon, while performing a movement to contact, discovers an NVA base camp and attacks it. Describe what you would have done differently if anything.

The A/2-14 IN Reading Discussion Questions

"My intent was for each lieutenant to respond online and then to use that as a springboard for our face-to-face discussion. I'll use the discussion that went along with the last question—*The Jungle, Question 2*—as an example:

comment: **The Jungle, Question 2**	(1 / 5) Posted: 04-29-2004
On 16 Nov 67, LT Downs platoon, while performing a movement to contact, discovers an NVA base camp and attacks it. Describe what you would have done differently if anything.	

"The first lieutenant to respond states that he would not have done anything differently, although he does make note of a lack of rear security:

comment: **RE: The Jungle, Question 2**	(2 / 5) Posted: 05-09-2004
I don't know if I would have done anything differently. It was a successful attack, they killed the enemy, gather some intel without losing any soldier. The only thing i didn't see was rear security. Every soldier had their weapon pointed toward the enemy, which means there were no rear security.	

"The next lieutenant to respond confirms that Lieutenant Downs was tactically sound in his attack. I liked the fact that both of these lieutenants were thinking through current light infantry tactics and comparing their understanding with what Lieutenant Downs did.

---

comment: RE: The Jungle, Question 2   (3 / 5) Posted: 05-09-2004

I can't say I would have done anything differently. From the description it seems that he was tactically sound in his attack of the location. It would help to have a visual picture of the attack, but he seemed to have an over watch element and an attack element. He also had his squads clearing bunkers and searching the structures. They then did a good job of searching the area and collecting the PIR. They then searched the area and establish a hasty defensive position. I can say I would have don't anything different.

"The third lieutenant, having read the previous responses, starts with 'Yes—BUT…' He identifies what he sees as a critical error: Lieutenant Downs initiated the attack with a voice command, which is a departure from the well-established infantry principle of initiating an attack with your most casualty producing weapon.

Answer: RE: The Jungle, Question 2   (4 / 5) Posted: 05-11-2004

Yes. BUT, I would never initiate a Platoon attack or an ambush of with a voice command. He should not have yelled "fire" even though that appears to be his preferred technique for initiating an attack.
Though LT Downs encountered a numerically superior force, his instinctive and decisive leadership carried his Platoon into a fight I would have entered as well under the same circumstances...but only the exact same. He flawlessly and fluidly executed Battle Drills 2 and 1 in rapid succession.
This is why I think that: His routes, approach, formations, actions at the security halt, "leader's recon" (kinda sorta by force), unit's use of effective hand and arm signals, simoultaneaous / fluid / completely effective emplacement of personnel as well as key weapons systems without being detected from a range of less than 10-100 meters, and unintended approach to the OBJ proved perfect in the movement to contact.
If I had accomplished the same, while maintaining the elements of surprise and initiative, I would have engaged the enemy forces.
However, I would have initiated the attack with my weapon system (and before the round had left my barrel I'd expect both guns to open). Of course, attempting to initiate with a claymore would be unrealistic considering this situation's particular METT-T. Remarks Complete.

"This kind of critical analysis is exactly what I was hoping for—it invites others to question, and it creates windows of opportunity for future conversation. The gem that would be the focus of our follow up face-to-face discussion came in the final comment:

---

comment: RE: The Jungle, Question 2   (5 / 5) Posted: 05-12-2004

i think that lt downs and his platoon did a good job on this mission. i can't see any major things that i would change. they set up a hasty attack and used the element surprise to help them gain superiorty. they attacked and cleared and set up a defesive position to defend against a counterattack. the only other thing he could have done was call in artilary or air strike.

"As with the previous three questions, I met with my four lieutenants during a meal and informally talked about what we had learned from the chapter. I started this discussion off by asking, 'Did anyone catch the last part of Lieutenant J's comment: "The only other thing he could have done was call in artillery or an air strike"? I'm wondering what you guys thought about that?' That question launched us into a phenomenal conversation that included more questions. For example, 'What if things hadn't gone well for Lieutenant Downs on the objective?' and 'What other assets did he have available?' Questions like this led us to insights about the value of integrating all available assets, including indirect fires, into platoon operations. In the conversation, we made connections and saw things that we had not seen in our individual readings of the book. It felt like a breakthrough of sorts—and I left that session knowing that if we went to combat, my lieutenants were better prepared than they were before.

"Part-way through this reading program experience, we were alerted to deploy to Iraq. As I write this, we are engaged in combat operations. I consider our reading program to be one factor in our success on the ground. For example, it helped give us a common reference point. It also helped my officers think deeper than just direct fire and maneuver of their forces. It taught them to use helicopters, recon assets, and anything else to avoid sending a man to do the job of a bullet. At the same time, it also taught them how one officer took his fight to the enemy, something that we have used several times. When we conduct split operations, when we have 'free radicals on the battlefield,' or when we sense complacency settling in—we have a depth of shared understanding as a direct result of *The Killing Zone* conversations.

"I also think that reading this particular book helped connect my lieutenants with former Soldiers, which showed how we are part of a time-honored profession that is bigger than just ourselves. As we are finding, some lessons in war are timeless."

Unpacking the Stories

Leader teams seem to get the most out of professional reading when they combine reading a relevant book with face-to-face and written conversation. In the next chapter, we'll go into greater depth about the transformative power of conversation. Here, we want to underscore the importance of choosing content that maps directly to your training goals.

Tips for Taking the *Pro-Reading Challenge*

- Select a relevant book that reinforces what you are trying to accomplish in your unit.
- Identify two-three insights that you would like to see your team walk away from the experience with. Hone in on the parts of the book that develop these insights. Use your reading selections to emphasize those parts of the book and then craft questions that will spark conversation in those same areas.
- Establish a clear timeline and clear expectations up front.
- Order the book (or get copies of the article) well ahead of time, so that it arrives one month in advance.
- Personally give the participants their copy of the book, writing a personal note in the book. Let them know how important you think the program is for each person as well as for the collective unit.
- Start off each week's discussion with a team huddle, perhaps over breakfast or lunch, and spark conversation about what participants are getting out of the book.
- Have a facilitator for your online discussion group who stimulates conversation or leads discussion on to new points. You can lead the discussions yourself or rotate the role among your leaders.
- Consider inviting members of the profession who are outside the reading group to participate in the online discussions. Try posting an open invitation online or inviting specific people to join in.
- Culminate the experience by having each participant reflect upon the one or two main things they are taking away from the experience and putting into action. Have them post this to the online space.
- (Also, see Chapter 9, "Making the Most of Online Conversations.")

Leaders who participate in the *Pro-Reading Challenge* are very intentional about choosing books that tie in with what they are trying to accomplish. They choose books that reinforce what they are already doing, and they situate the program and the conversations in the "now" experiences of their leaders. In other words, they focus their leaders on the "So what, how does this apply to us as a unit?"

Todd Schmidt, for example, wanted his leaders to gain insight into the culture, history, and religion of the region they would be operating in. *Taliban* met his intent. Scott Shaw had a more tactical focus; he chose a book that was chock-full of the same dilemmas that today's rifle platoon leaders face. Another company commander, George Corbari, wanted to raise his team's overall effectiveness. He selected *The 21 Irrefutable Laws of Leadership* by John Maxwell. Thus, there is no one type of book that is best. The key is to be very intentional about your book choices and to integrate the reading into the current reality of your unit.

A pro-reading program that focuses on highly relevant content offers four notable benefits:

1. It creates a shared experience

When a leader team reads and talks about the same book, the ideas and language in the book become a shared experience that the team draws upon in the future. For example, discussing *The Killing Zone* enabled Scott Shaw and his lieutenants to be transported to the 1960s Vietnam that Fred Downs experienced. Specific experiences, insights, and even words serve as a sort of shorthand that is laden with the deeper meanings that emerged from their conversations. In Iraq, Scott can ask his platoon leaders if they have brought to bear all available assets and refer to Lieutenant Downs' NVA base camp attack. It's not just the example from the book, but the insights prompted by the discussions that are invoked when Scott refers to this attack.

Todd Schmidt also created some amazing shared experiences for his team through reading and talking about the book *Taliban,* listening to experts talk about the culture and history of Afghanistan, and experiencing the culture through its food, music, and incense. When they encountered shifting loyalties on the ground in Afghanistan, Todd's leaders had a more nuanced view of what was happening as a result of their book discussions. Having a shared frame of reference around critical issues is what separates good teams from great teams.

All of us have had the experience of being surprised when someone else drew very different conclusions from reading the same book we read. It causes us to think, "Did I miss something?" "Why didn't I see that?" This is a great stimulus for making new mental connections as was evident in the example that Scott Shaw described, in which his lieutenants commented on what Lieutenant Downs had done. Differences in interpretation like this then become fertile ground for making new connections—causing us to rethink our assumptions and broaden our perspectives.

Discussing concrete situations that occurred in a book allows a team to be openly critical in ways that might be uncomfortable if the subject were a situation in which team members had been participants. Analyzing a mistake that Lieutenant Downs made is easy for the team to discuss—not so when the mistake was made by one of the lieutenants on the team.

2. It helps people retain knowledge

Discussion improves our ability to retain what we have read. How often have you read an article, but then three days later were unable to remember anything except a vague impression of what it was about? If, however, you had told your spouse about it, or made yourself some notes, or had a discussion with someone else who had read it, you would have increased the staying power of the ideas in the book tenfold. Three weeks later you would probably not remember the whole article, but you would very likely remember what you said in the discussion, the points you made, and the points that the other person made that surprised you. Research in learning shows that unless you "recall" (that is pull back into conscious memory) what you have learned within 24 hours, you will lose most of it. Todd Schmidt touched on this when he noted that the discussions caused people "to think deeper about what they were learning."

3. It builds a sense of professional identity

Reading relevant materials such as military history creates a historical bond with our predecessors. It also creates a lateral bond with our fellow professionals, as we gain a shared understanding of who we are as members of this profession. For example, conversations about *Leadership, The Warrior's Art* among the HHC/1-509th (ABN) leaders sparked local conversations throughout the Army.

The content of the reading and the lateral connections with other members of the profession are key factors in creating a sense of professional community. So, too, are the physical aspects of the program. Chris Kolenda provided the extra touch that makes an impact when he personalized each book with an inscription. George Corbari told us that when he was a lieutenant, his company commander inscribed a copy of *A Message For Garcia* for him. The book took on much greater meaning for him over the years because of the inscription. When he did the same for his officers, George was passing on this legacy, and reinforcing the sense of being part of something greater than ourselves. CC provides a similar, though admittedly less personal, physical link between professionals when it supplies groups with books of their choice. Members of reading groups can hold up a copy of a book and say, "This was given to me by CC and inscribed by my commander." In effect, the book represents their membership in the profession; it becomes their link to the past and the future.

4. It amplifies the impact of the learning

Leaders like Todd Schmidt, Scott Shaw, and George Corbari are leveraging the *Pro-Reading Challenge* to develop leaders and to improve their unit's effectiveness. In addition to making it easier for them to accomplish their goals, the *Pro-Reading Challenge* amplifies what they are doing by making it visible to the rest of the profession through the online discussion. Leaders across the 1-509th (ABN), for example, were given access to thinking and insights about leadership that otherwise would have been hidden to them.

Just as these small groups have an impact on the wider profession as their conversation is amplified via the online space, so too does the wider profession influence the smaller group. The act of writing one's thoughts down—declaring what you think—is valuable in itself. But it takes on new meaning when you know others will be reading what you think. Participants tend to be more thoughtful in their discussion posts knowing that their peers and other members of the profession may read what they write.

*****

Our desire is that this chapter inspires you to use professional reading—fueled by conversation—as an integral part of how you develop your leaders and increase your unit's effectiveness. Additionally, if you are working in the capacity of a topic lead or professional forum developer, this chapter makes the case that professional forums can directly impact professional reading by providing resources and online space for leaders to "do" professional reading more effectively.

Key Concepts—Chapter 3

- A growing number of leaders are using professional reading as a catalyst for conversations within their units—shifting the emphasis from the reading to the conversation about the reading.

- When leader teams read relevant content together, the conversations that result shift individual learning curves and so improve unit effectiveness.

- Combining face-to-face and online conversation about the reading increases the impact of a reading program, with four notable benefits:

  1. It creates a shared experience which catalyzes insightful discussion and acts as a point of reference in later situations.

  2. It improves knowledge retention through the process of conversation, which includes reflection and articulation of what is being learned.

  3. It builds a sense of professional identity by creating lateral connections with fellow readers as well as historical bonds with past warriors.

  4. It amplifies the impact of the learning by making both the individual and the profession at large aware of the learning taking place.

Chapter 4

Conversations That Shape Us

"Child Dies, Deployment Pending"

Just days ago you learned that the only child of one of your NCOs passed away from a long-term illness. This terrible incident has come at a difficult time—your unit is preparing to deploy to OIF 2 in three months. You are the Company Commander, and you have little experience handling issues of death and bereavement. You face a number of difficult dilemmas. First, naturally you are concerned about his and the family's well-being. What kind of support team will you create to take care of the family now and while you are deployed? Second, the NCO holds an important position in the company. He is well-respected and a valuable member of your company, and you must make a decision regarding his deployment status. During a conversation with the NCO, he expresses his dedication to the unit and tells you he wants to deploy. What do you do?

This scenario, created by Chris Engen based on his own personal experience, was posted to the *Command Challenge* section of CompanyCommand.army.mil.[1] In this chapter we use the online discussion that took place about "A Child Dies, Deployment Pending" as a window into understanding how conversations transform the thinking of the company commanders who are involved in them.

---

[1] *Command Challenges* place members in a leadership scenario in which they analyze a situation, rate the available options, and then discuss their thinking with other members. CC members develop and submit the challenges based on their own experiences leading Soldiers. For more insight into the theory behind this idea, read *Practical Intelligence in Everyday Life* (Sternberg, et al., 2000).

But first, some background on how this *Command Challenge* originated.

Chris Engen's Reflections

"While I was a company commander, I had a junior sergeant who lost a child right before we were to be deployed. Everyone was looking to me for guidance about what decisions we were going to make regarding the sergeant and his family. I felt very comfortable in most aspects of company command, but when it came to this kind of personal crisis-type situation, I felt kind of inadequate to the task, especially without the frame of reference of having a child of my own. That whole process was pretty challenging. When I look back on it, I don't know if I would have done things differently, but I felt that I never really had the tools to turn to. Since that experience, I've always wondered if there was something we could do to help other company commanders with issues of death and grief—something that's not talked about all that much in our leadership training. However, I wasn't sure if it was just my own personal experience that was causing me to think this was important or if it really was a leadership issue that needed to be addressed.

"I had been involved with CC for a long while and had participated in several *Command Challenges*, so I decided that if I was going to find out how significant this issue was, CC was the place it was going to happen. I would get answers directly from the source, from experienced company commanders. The challenge that went up on the site looked like this:

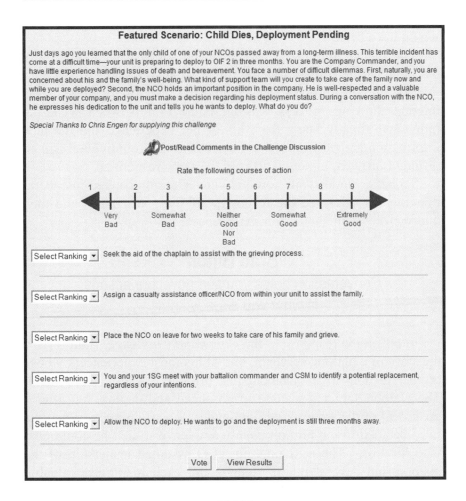

*****

More than 700 CC members participated in the "Child Dies, Deployment Pending" *Command Challenge*. In addition to reading the scenario and rating the options, twenty-five members also posted written responses in the challenge discussion area. Most of these responses were three to five paragraphs long, and many related a similar event that the writer had experienced.

Did the conversation change the thinking of the people involved? Perhaps the most obvious conclusion to draw is that it didn't provide what we typically think of as answers. The readers of others' comments did not say to themselves, "Now I have the answer!" or "Now I see the light!" However, the conversation did produce change in the thinking of individuals that participated in it, change that was more subtle and more profound than answers would have been.

The change in thinking was produced not by what another said, but by what the readers *thought* about what was said. It was their internal thinking process that created the insights for them. This internal thinking process was an interaction between what the individual already knew from his or her experience and the new information gained from the conversation. Each individual gained different insights, although all read the same responses.

To better understand how the conversation changed members' thinking, we analyzed the responses of five participants and then interviewed them about their experiences.

Brad Hilton
Conversation helps you see new connections in what you already know.

In his online response to the *Command Challenge*, Brad related the story of a platoon sergeant, one of his most experienced, whose brother died in a car accident just prior to a major deployment. The platoon sergeant wanted to go ahead and deploy, but after a great deal of discussion with him and with various support people, Brad decided to put him on emergency leave so that he could deal with his loss. The next ranking NCO assumed leadership of the platoon and several others stepped up, each making a valuable contribution. As it turned out, the platoon sergeant had not fully realized that he needed to grieve; even though he resisted being sent home at the time, he was grateful afterward. Brad concluded his story by saying:

> I learned the value in preparing for the loss of key leaders and learned that it also included me! I started practicing what I was then preaching and started training my XO to assume command quickly in case something happened to me. I ended up missing a few weeks during my command because of a very personal family tragedy. The troop XO did extremely well in my absence, which I attribute in large part to the lesson I learned above.

Long before the "Child Dies" *Command Challenge* went up on the site, this was a topic to which Brad had given considerable thought. He had, in fact, related the lessons of his platoon sergeant's experience many times when coaching junior leaders and company commanders. But, participating in the *Command Challenge* conversation changed the way he thought about this issue. Brad notes:

> Previously, when I've told this story of my NCO whose brother died, I never mentioned that piece where I too was gone for a week and the XO took over. Before this *Command Challenge*, I had just not connected that event to the lesson I had learned with my platoon sergeant. Somehow the connection was made for me by what Nate Allen and Rob Griggs wrote in the online discussion. What they wrote must have hit an emotional button somewhere because I read the *Challenge* at the end of the day when I was ready to go home, yet I sat there for an hour and typed out my response. Reading their comments and then writing out my own experience reshaped how I would go forward in the future. In a mentoring role about this subject, I would now include the part about myself and say, "By the way, in addition to preparing for subordinate leader absences, you also have to prepare for your own possible absence."

Writing out his own response leads Brad to an important insight. All the facts for that insight were available to him before the *Challenge*, but it takes the stimulus of the conversation for him to connect the facts into a valuable insight. People think in a different way when they are putting together the logic they will use to help others understand their position, as opposed to when they are simply mulling over their position in their own minds. The process of formulating a response in conversation—written or oral—benefits the writer/speaker as well as the reader/listener because it creates connections and learning that otherwise would not happen.

Rob Griggs
Conversation gives you insight into others' reasoning.

Although Rob Griggs' online response to the *Challenge* was relatively brief, it was often referenced by other participants. "As an effective company commander, you should be able to manage the company dealing with the loss of any soldier," Rob noted. Later he said, "Let the NCO do what he needs to do for as long as he needs to do it." Like others, he recounted a brief experience of his own, related to his father-in-law's death, and sympathized with the experiences of others.

When asked how reading others' responses impacted his own thinking, Rob says,

> When this *Command Challenge* was initially posted, I voted to keep the sergeant back—and my decision wouldn't be any different after participating in the discussion. However, my understanding of the NCO's desire to deploy, and the ramifications of my decision to keep him back are enhanced. Let's say, for example, the sergeant in this scenario came to me and said, "Listen sir, I know you are saying that you don't want me to deploy; however, if you'll just give me a few weeks to grieve, then I'd like to join the unit." If I had not participated in the *Command Challenge*, my response would have been, "Listen, I know what you're saying, but you're wrong." But, I wouldn't have a good basis for understanding what he was going through—I wouldn't have Nate's perspective on losing a kid; I wouldn't have Chris' point of view. After being part of the discussion, I would still say, "I want to give you more time than that"— but I would better understand.
>
> I would be able to dialogue with the NCO and say, "Listen, I understand what you are saying," and I *would* understand it because his perspective was laid out on the Web site in front of me. It's a better way for me to interact with that sergeant, to have some understanding of his point of view.

By participating in the *Command Challenge* conversation, Rob has to clarify his own position in order to communicate it, but he also gains insight into the reasoning of other people. He feels that this insight would enable him to hold a different kind of conversation with the sergeant, one that would be more empathetic and genuine. What is often most useful for the reader of an online conversation is not the specific answers or positions others take, but rather understanding the logic and reasoning that supports their positions. This understanding leads the reader to a new level of insight.

Traci Cook
Conversation broadens your perspective.

Traci, who is the topic lead for the *FRG Leader* forum, also responded with a personal story. Hers was about the death of her younger brother and the realization that it took her mother more than two years to again "resemble the mother I've known all my life." Writing from her perspective as an FRG leader, she advised involving the FRG and providing long-term assistance to the family. "Grieving doesn't go away after the funeral," she says.

For Traci, reading what others had written raises issues she had not considered. Her initial thinking, focused on how it feels to lose someone, was "Just don't send him at all." But some of the discussion causes her to give credence to what she thought of as the "military view," that is the importance of the mission, and also the idea that the NCO may have reasons to deploy that she had not thought about. She says, "After all, he's an adult who has to consider both his family and his future career. So after reading others' comments, I could see reasons why he should be deployed."

Participating in the *Command Challenge* conversation broadens Traci's view, adding a perspective that hadn't occurred to her. And, beyond simply hearing another's perspective, she gives credence to it, seeing it as a legitimate position.

Tony Burgess
Conversation helps you question your own assumptions.

Tony Burgess had worked with Chris early in the development of the *Challenge*. His initial response to the question was that the sergeant should not deploy, feeling that he was not in any shape to deploy and doing so would undermine his family relationships as well as the unit's effectiveness. In the course of working with Chris to package the *Challenge* and then reading the early online responses, Tony found that his initial thinking did not change.

After the "Child Dies" *Command Challenge* had been up on the site for a couple of weeks, Chris decided to hold a "live huddle," which would be an online synchronous meeting (or chat) about the challenge. During the "live huddle," Chris made a statement that led to an insight for Tony. Chris said, "One option may be to facilitate, but delay his departure. Keep him home for the first 3-6 months. Establish means to monitor the family. If support is there and working, he then deploys."

That comment caused Tony to realize that his past experience had put an unnecessary constraint on his thinking. He writes:

> Before 2003, Army deployments were shorter and more "all or nothing" as far as who you took with you. For example, I deployed to Saudi Arabia for 6 months and there was no option to come over halfway through—we just didn't think that way. But now, with year-long deployments, other options are possible—I didn't see them because of an un-recognized self-imposed time limit that I had in my mind.

Tony then posted this response in the "Child Dies, Deployment Pending" discussion area:

> During a "live huddle" we had here on CC.com, where we talked about this *Command Challenge*, Chris Engen brought up something that I found helpful: Instead of thinking in terms of "all or nothing" with this NCO—which is what I was doing initially—i.e., either he deploys with the unit

or he doesn't—there is the option of having him deploy sometime after the unit has departed. For example, the NCO might need 3-6 months before he is reasonably ready to deploy. Given that our deployments are running at a year, this is a good option to have available.

Participating in the live huddle allows Tony to become aware of an assumption that he is basing his view on. When he becomes aware of the assumption, he is able to evaluate its validity. Chris does not point out this assumption to Tony; rather, Chris' comment allows Tony to recognize it for himself.

Chris Engen
Conversation highlights gaps between your own views and those of other professionals.

Earlier, Chris described why he created this *Challenge* scenario. Here he explains how he thought about the *Challenge* before participating in the discussion.

> If the NCO felt he was ready and he wanted to go on deployment, I would have taken him on the deployment, but I would have utilized the chaplain, other counseling resources, and the family support group to make sure that the needs of the family were met.

Reading others' responses, however, gave Chris a surprise:

> One of the things that surprised me in the conversation was the number of people who said, at the drop of the hat, "leave him back." They seemed to give no thought to the impact on the unit. And that surprised me a little because, while I would want to do everything to care for the individual and his family, I personally felt a need to somehow fulfill my obligation as a unit commander. My thought is when we volunteer for service in the army, we are making a commitment and there is a

lot of personal sacrifice that comes with that. Sometimes we don't always get to do the things we might want to do because of that commitment. It's part of raising your right hand and saying you'll do the job. We say, "mission first," yet here were all these people putting the soldier before the mission.

This surprise causes Chris to question his own thinking. His questioning leads him to the idea that he voiced in the live huddle and that affected Tony Burgess' thinking. By the end of the conversation Chris has come to a new position:

> I'm still committed to the mission, but I started to look at, rather than a black and white situation, more options—so that it doesn't have to be that he immediately deploys vs. he stays back for a year, but strike a balance, like he only deploys for 6 months—something like that. I still want to achieve the mission, but realize that there were a lot of people out there that had some good insights and powerful things to say about keeping him back.

Surprise at the distance between his views and those of others' leads Chris to become aware of what he calls "black and white thinking" and to search for a more balanced position. So, although others' views do not provide this insight for him, without the views of others, he cannot re-frame his own position.

In other words, the conversation creates cognitive dissonance for Chris. Since the others who are offering surprising or opposing ideas are fellow professionals, Chris cannot easily dismiss them. Dissonance like this can be particularly strong when you know and respect the other person. The conflict created by the differing views causes Chris to seek a new way to look at the situation, finding a new position that allows both positions to exist simultaneously.

Unpacking the Stories

The stories illustrate five ways that conversation influences the thinking of CC members. Conversation:

- Helps you see new connections in what you already know,
- Gives you insight into others' reasoning,
- Broadens your perspective,
- Helps you question your own assumptions, and
- Highlights gaps between your own views and those of other professionals.

These ways of learning from conversation are often unintentional. In this example, Chris Engen initiated the *Challenge* because he wanted to know if others also saw the lack of bereavement advice and tools as a problem. But, in addition to getting an answer to that question, like many of the other members, he also gained knowledge he had not intentionally sought out.

By and large, members did not participate in the *Command Challenge* intending to gain a specific answer. Yet all were open to the learning that did occur for them. In the follow-up interviews, they spoke of being curious about what others had to say on the issue, which led them to read what other people had written. In a broad sense, they came with the intention to learn by calibrating their own thinking against others' thinking.

*****

A single conversation is like the proverbial pebble in a pond—its impact expands in ever-widening circles. Many of those who responded to the "Child Dies" *Challenge* online also held conversations off-line. For example, Rob Griggs talked about the topic with his father who had been a first sergeant in Viet Nam, and Traci Cook talked to her husband, Nate, about it. Considering the 700 members who participated directly and the thousands who read from the periphery, this one conversation could easily have resulted in hundreds, even thousands, of conversations in units across the Army: "Hey did you see that *Command Challenge* about a Soldier's child dying just before a major deployment? What did you think?"

If we were to multiply the learning from every conversation that occurs on CC and add to that number the off-line conversations that reverberate, the capability of conversation to unleash the power of the Army profession is inspiring.

Key Concepts—Chapter 4

- Conversations transform the thinking of the company commanders involved in them.

- Conversation does not supply what is typically thought of as "answers;" rather, it causes participants to think, and it is this internal thinking process that creates insights for those involved in the conversation.

- Although participants in online conversations read the same discussion comments, each gains unique insights.

- Online conversations extend far beyond the Web site to inspire a multitude of informal discussions.

Chapter 5

Finding the Heart of the Profession

The preceding chapters paint a picture of members actively engaging in the central activities of a professional forum: connecting in conversations, creating and sharing knowledge, and becoming more effective as a result. Such a high level of member participation is vital; without it, forums like CC cannot thrive.

Given the critical need for members to step up to leadership roles within the forum, it is important to ask, "How do members of the profession become more actively involved in CC?"

The stories of four CC team members, told in their own words, provide an important glimpse into this process.

Rob Thornton

Rob commanded both A/1-24 IN and HHC/1-24 IN—part of the 1st Brigade, 25th ID Stryker Brigade Combat Team (SBCT) at Fort Lewis, Washington. He is a topic lead for both the SBCT and the Unit of Action (UA) rally points.

"About the time you hit the Captain's Career Course, you're fired up about getting a command and you have some time to get yourself ready. I think I first heard about CompanyCommand.com from one of my buddies in the course. I started looking at it and I downloaded some things I liked. I didn't really answer anything, and I didn't think I had anything to give at the time. I started regularly visiting the site when I got to Fort Lewis, about a year before command. I was asking myself, 'What things are going to be critical to my success that I can get done now before I take command?' For example, there were no SBCT (Stryker Brigade Combat Team) company commander TACSOPs—there was a battalion TACSOP, but none for company level. I downloaded the ones that were available and started piecemealing one together that I thought would give me a good start.

"I started following a couple of the conversations and taking a look at products that earlier I had not seen as applicable. Although I was in the site more often, I didn't really participate because by now I was consumed with being a staff officer. And I guess I felt hesitant about contributing, not having been a company commander.

"In June of 2002, I took command of Alpha Company 1-24 IN (STRYKER). I think I might have weighed in on a discussion thread then, but I was really busy producing my own products. I did send in the TACSOP I'd developed because I'd taken so many TACSOPs off the site, and I thought I should give back what I took out. Instead of participating much with CompanyCommand.com, my energy went into building the products I needed to help me get through the initial phases of transformation. As those products began to work, I began sending them to my buddies over the local area network. I got back a lot of feedback about how much it helped them.

"It was about this time that Tony came up to Ft. Lewis and sat in on one of our brigade leader development seminars. He told me that he was coming up and would like to meet with me after the seminar. He asked if I wanted to host the SBCT commander rally point. The reason he asked me, he said, was because I had told him that the information I needed for my SBCT company was almost non-existent.

"Tony said that if I started an *SBCT* rally point, I could put information out there that was relevant and useful to guys who were having to work through the problems associated with transformation. That made sense to me because, by the time Tony asked me, I already had quite a few tools and some stories and other stuff that I had accumulated. Collecting products and lessons learned and reflecting on my experiences is part of the way I work, so I agreed to lead the rally point.

"I had been a topic lead for about six months when we had a meeting of all the CompanyCommand topic leads in D.C. That was a turning point in terms of my own growth as a topic lead. The meeting made a big difference by putting a face on the names of the other topic leads, and it helped me see the connection between the different sections of CompanyCommand.army.mil. Now I'm more likely to weigh in on a discussion in other topics and to establish links between my sections and others. One of the things that changed for me, as a result of this meeting, was being more 'real' on the site. It was something Nate said at that meeting that I really didn't understand at first: 'You have to bring yourself to the table.' Talking with Tony about that later helped clarify it for me. 'You can put some of yourself in this so they get to know you,' Tony said. I thought, 'I do that every day with the people in my company.' When I thought of it that way, what Nate had said earlier made perfect sense.

"The idea of 'being real' has significantly changed how I interact on the site. I've started sharing some of my own experiences on the SBCT main page and sending personal emails to contributors who send in something I really connect with. It has allowed me to be me.

"As I become more senior, more professionally mature, I have a greater desire to have an impact on the profession—not only because I care about it and I care about the Soldiers, but also because I'm going to continue to work inside this profession. If you believe in something, you want to have an impact on it because it's going to come back to you at some point. So I ask myself, 'What direction are we taking our profession?' You could ask that about your company, your battalion, about the Web site, about the army. In the same way that you are an active participant in shaping the government when you vote, you have the opportunity to be actively involved in shaping this profession."

Traci Cook

Traci led the B/1-39 FA (MLRS) family readiness group at Fort Stewart, Georgia. She is a topic lead for the FRG leader forum.

"When my husband, Nate, took command at Fort Stewart in March 2001, I assumed the leadership of his unit's FRG (Family Readiness Group). I was always on the lookout for resources to help me be a better leader of families. When Nate introduced me to CompanyCommand.com, which he used for command information, I was instantly impressed. I read everything on the site, starting with Cathy Speer's article, "5 Minutes on Family Readiness," which summarized the main mission of FRGs for commanders. I found some tools on the site that I could use, and I was thankful that I would not have to reinvent everything myself; but, I also saw that it was difficult to find useful ideas. I remember thinking that this Web site has the potential to be a really powerful tool—but it's not there yet!

"I would check the FRG page periodically to see if there was a new discussion or new information, but didn't participate in any of the discussions because I wasn't sure that what I had to say would be useful to others. I guess I just wanted to be a little more anonymous. It was also a time issue for me; I like to craft what I say before I put it out there and I didn't have the time then. But then in September 2002, when my husband changed out of command, I had a little more free time on my hands. I thought, I've learned a lot about being an FRG leader, so I wrote an article ("Guide for Commander's Spouses for Those First Few Weeks in Command") and sent it in. I got back this really amazing message from Pete Kilner that began with, 'Are you a professional writer? This is really well written! Have you written some other things you could send in?' I was so encouraged by his feedback that I started sending in a new article about once a month. I also approached Pete with the idea of a book for FRG leaders with tips, ideas, and tools. He responded with, 'Why not use this Web site as an initial draft of ideas?' which encouraged me to create even more content for the site.

"Pete then introduced me to Tony Burgess and he and I started emailing as well. In April, Tony asked me if I'd consider being one of the topic leads for the FRG page. He connected me with Cathy Speer who had been working on the site for some time.

"I've had a lot of support from the whole team, and I'm thrilled now to have a partner in Angela Crist. Every time Angela and I have asked a question—and we've had a lot of questions—we get an immediate response from someone on the team, so I never feel like I'm on my own. For example, during the DC trip, Jamie Chanez really helped me focus on how to market the site to FRG leaders. From these ideas, Angela and I have produced a great brochure. For me, the great thing about working on the FRG forum is that they kept saying, 'Just go and run with it,' so I have the freedom to really invent some new things for FRG leaders. Amazingly, the CC team's enthusiasm has not waned; they are no less encouraging now than they were two years ago when I took on the role of topic lead. Now I find myself modeling that encouragement and affirmation when FRG leaders send in ideas and stories to me.

"I think FRG leaders have a real need for this kind of information. The FRG topic is growing each day. We are continuously looking for new directions to go in and new ways to be useful to this community. This experience has been a great developmental opportunity for me as well. For example, I accompanied the team to Schofield Barracks, HI in March 2003 to meet with the FRG leaders there whose spouses were getting ready to deploy to combat. The responses I've had from those leaders and others who have come to the site have let me know I'm really making a difference for FRG leadership."

Rob Mitchell

Rob commanded the 744th EOD company at Fort Meade, Maryland—a command that included combat operations in Afghanistan (OEF 1). He is a topic lead for the EOD rally point.

"I knew about CompanyCommand.com because I had been on the site and had participated in some of the discussions while I was an EOD (Explosive Ordnance Disposal) company commander. CompanyCommand.com covers a fairly wide breadth of the Army and although there was nothing specific to EOD on the site, there was a lot of general information about leadership that I found very helpful, particularly for a junior officer.

"When I came out of command and went to teach at the EOD School at Eglin Air Force Base, Florida, I said to myself, 'The EOD community needs to come together more often.' EOD is a unique branch; we have some 40 company commanders that are spread out across the entire continental landmass to do bomb-squad type missions. We rarely meet as a group more than once every year because of the geographic separation. Yet, when we have gotten together, there is an enormous amount that we learn from each other. I had been thinking for some time that EOD company commanders needed a bulletin board or some site where we could have a true professional discussion of items of interest to the field. I'm not the most altruistic person, but I wanted to make the future of this career field that I love a lot a better place for my successors.

"When I moved to Florida, I started thinking about how we could make that happen. CompanyCommand.com was the most likely place that I could think of; it was the one frame of reference that most of us had. This would have been in 2002 and nothing else really existed at the time. Of course, the CompanyCommand.com site was a good deal more simplistic then. But it did have the same positive approach back then and that was important to me because I didn't want to start a gripe session, but rather a genuine professional forum.

"I hit Tony up about it—well, actually I begged him to let me put an EOD section on CompanyCommand.com. We talked about it a number of times and emailed back and forth with him asking me questions that gave me some good food for thought:

- What would the purpose be?
- Where would it be six months from now?
- Who do you know that you could enlist to help?
- Does your present job give you time to do it?

"What I understand now is that Tony was asking me about the key factors that he knew would make it successful. I was able to answer those questions positively, so he gave me the page and said, 'Run with it.'

"Now I had a site and I was also fortunate to have 16 EOD commanders in training at the time who served as a sounding board. I said to them, 'I'm going to set up this EOD site and you guys see what you think.' These officers participated in the forum and got a lot out of it—its popularity was pretty evident. With that success behind me, I then went to all the EOD commanders I knew and said, 'Hey, I'm doing this thing, take a look see.' We are a small group in EOD, so the word spread very quickly and again I got a lot of very positive feedback.

"I then started a section called *War Stories* that I use to draw people in. If you think about a magazine cover, you put the sexy stuff on the top so people will go in a little further. The war stories are people giving their first-hand, fireside chat accounts of something harrowing or amusing that happened to them—like one titled 'Just another close call in Iraq.' When I check in with commanders and ask, 'Hey, have you read that?' They say, 'Yes, that's cool, we ought to have more like that.'

"I draw them in the door with the war stories and then when they click on the AAR section they see something that may be relevant to them right now as a company commander. The AARs have spurred a lot of dialogue between outgoing and incoming commanders. Someone outgoing will post an AAR and someone on a future rotation will see it and think to themselves, 'Hey, I hadn't thought about that; I need to flesh that out a little bit more.' Then, they'll email the outgoing commander and start a one-on-one discussion. Although we have some online discussions on the Web site, I am most pleased about those dynamic, behind-the-scenes conversations.

"As the CC team told me when I started, you have to keep trying new things. I have found it interesting how people actually participate. I can email EOD commanders a survey with a question like, 'What problems with supply accountability/ automation have you experienced, and what solutions have you come up with?' And overnight I get 25 or more responses. As a result, I've become a big fan of surveys; I send one out probably every three months on a topic that is of current interest. Then I post the responses over the next couple of months.

"I've also noticed that participation fluctuates a lot—sometimes it picks up and sometimes it drops off. I think participation is a function of how busy we are. For example, EOD is extremely busy during an election year, because we provide support to the election candidates. So in the months before an election, my participation percentage will be low.

"Back in 2002 I thought I could get a professional dialogue started. Two years later, I'm still learning how to do that, trying out different ideas, but I know I'm having an impact."

Jay Miseli

Jay commanded both C/2-69 AR and HHC/2-69 AR at Fort Benning, Georgia—a command that included combat operations in Iraq (OIF 1). He is a topic lead for the HQ Commander rally point.

"I got to Fort Benning in August 2000 and found out I was going to take command of a tank company in November, so I had very little time to prepare for the job and become familiar with the battalion. Around October, I learned that the company didn't have a TACSOP so I did a Web search for tank company SOPs, and that took me to CompanyCommand.com. That was my first time on the site. I didn't find a tank company TACSOP, but I did find some other useful things like operations orders and a change-of-command inventory matrix. I downloaded these tools onto a disc, took them to work, and started reviewing them. Although I still wound up having to create my own TACSOP, the other stuff that I'd pulled off the site simplified my life enough that I could focus on developing my own SOP. I was able to tailor the command inventory stuff for my tank company and, as I found out later, that command inventory matrix kind of took on a life of its own. Then except for checking in intermittently, I pretty much fell off the net and planned to come back in when I got the tank SOP finished.

"I finally got the SOP finished in March and went back in to see what was on the site. There was still no tank company SOP, so I sent mine in. Chris Engen was the topic lead at the time and I got a very nice email from both him and Tony saying, 'Thanks, we're going to post it and do you have anything more?' That made me laugh, but I wrote back and said, 'No, not really.' But I did go in to look after it was posted—I guess I just wanted to make sure it was exactly what I wrote. I wound up thinking that it was really cool. I thought, 'Hey, I'm on the Web!' It was an awesome feeling to see it up there.

"Then I kind of unplugged from the site again because I had a National Training Center rotation and immediately following that I gave up command of the tank company and took over command of my headquarters company. I gave the guy who replaced me the change-of-command inventory tool that I had tailored for my tank company. I said, 'Look, I'm not telling you how to do the inventory, but this is one way you could do it.' He thought it was great and used it. I was also able to tailor it and use it for my headquarters company—so you can see that it was getting a lot of use. That was in August 2001, and a few weeks later, with 9-11, every facet of being in the Army changed!

"Our battalion was notified that we would deploy to Kuwait and a new commander was scheduled to take over the battalion in May 2002. He came to Fort Benning early in March to meet with the company commanders of the battalion to see what we were doing to get ready to deploy and to just kind of get a pulse of the organization. When he saw me, he said, 'Jay, I read your SOP— it's good!' And I thought, 'Wow, CompanyCommand.com has much broader exposure than I thought if a lieutenant colonel at Fort McPherson came across my SOP.' That really changed my view of the Web site, because, up until then, I had thought of it simply as a place where I could go to look for some tool I needed—at that point I realized it was much more than that.

"That next year was intense and included two deployments to Kuwait, with the second one ending in Baghdad! After the first deployment to Kuwait, I captured my deployment AAR and sent it in. During that time, I also found a great mechanized infantry HQ company SOP on CompanyCommand.com that I used to create my field trains SOP. I sent that product in also. After doing our 'business' in Iraq, in May 2003, I made it my mission to write my AAR before I left Baghdad. I knew that it was critical to capture what we had learned for others who would follow us. So, I sent in the AAR as well as a PowerPoint presentation that captured our convoy operations lessons learned.

"Submitting the PowerPoint presentation and my AAR to Tony from Kuwait was the turning point for my involvement in CompanyCommand.com. There were two things that were the tipping point for me. First, Tony attacked me! I mean I got multiple emails from Tony saying, 'We need to get you involved; we want you on the team.' But I was still reeling from coming back from Iraq, so I kind of put him off and said, 'That sounds interesting, we'll talk more.' But the thing that actually cemented it for me was an email I got from a headquarters company commander of a tank battalion in Korea—someone I didn't know—thanking me. He had downloaded my OIF AAR, and he had used it, not only to influence his organization, but through the chain of command, to influence how the brigade executed their logistics. Then it hit me, 'Okay, my battalion commander saw my SOP before he came a year ago—that's not really all that significant. But a tank brigade in Korea is going to be better equipped to fight if they're called—wow!' I was just floored that a document I wrote had this influence well outside of what I thought of as my relatively small sphere of influence. So, when I got back to the States and Tony hit me again—actually the email attack had never stopped—I'm like, 'Yeah, I'm on board.'

"The tank company TACSOP that originally brought me to CompanyCommand.com is still going. The company commander that took over the tank company from me came and left, and the next guy came. The new guy decided he wanted to revamp how they did business, so he and his first sergeant searched for TACSOPs on the Web and they downloaded the one I had written two years before and adopted it pretty much in its original form. So, there was that TACSOP again. The new commander would have never known about it without it being on CompanyCommand.com!"

Unpacking the Stories

Although there are many factors that foster involvement in the CC professional forum, three stand out in the preceding stories: Connection with members of the CC team, an intrinsic desire to make an impact on the profession, and the license to be creative.

Interactions with the CC team

The most prominent theme across the stories is the relationship that developed over time between the CC member and the CC team. Each of the storytellers describes multiple conversations he or she had with the CC team that eventually leads that individual to make a commitment to a leadership role. It is an iterative process that typically begins with the individual posting content or otherwise contributing. In so doing, the individual becomes visible to the team and, as a result, a member of the CC team initiates a conversation. The initial conversations are a mix of positive feedback and invitations to participate more. It seems to be both the frequency of the interactions as well as the content and tone of the messages that encourage these four members. Chris Engen, a topic lead at the time, writes Jay Miseli to thank him for his TACSOP and asks him if he has more content to share. Tony joins Chris in thanking Jay and invites him to continue making a difference for the profession. Traci Cook is thrilled by Pete's query, "Are you a professional writer?" and later she is encouraged by his suggestion to use the Web site as a draft for her potential book. Pete introduces Traci to Tony who invites her to play a more active role with the team.

There is a pattern of multiple members of the CC team developing a relationship with these members that creates a richer relationship and a deeper level of understanding and trust. For Rob Thornton, Nate's talking about bringing himself to the table (during the meeting in D.C.), becomes meaningful only after he talks with Tony about the same thing, relating it to his own experience commanding a company. Rob does not dismiss the new idea when he first hears it from Nate, but neither does he fully integrate it into his own thinking until he hears it from a different perspective. In Rob's case, several different voices across these ongoing conversations deepen his understanding, as well as his relationship with the CC team. It is important that the greater CC team be actively involved in communicating with members—creating synergy and a broader impact—rather than one person on the team having this role.

Many of the storytellers talk about initially being unsure that they have anything to contribute or about not wanting to hold themselves up as experts. They experience the frequent and supportive communication with the CC team as a validation of their contributions. This communication gives them, in a sense, permission to contribute. In the stories, members are reassured that their contributions are on target. Although Jay laughs at the audacity of Chris and Tony asking him for more content, he takes it as an affirmation that his TACSOP is useful and, when he does develop something else, he is predisposed to post it.

In addition to ongoing conversations via phone calls and email, meeting members in person is a significant part of developing a strong relationship. Rob Thornton mentions Tony's visit to Fort Lewis as the catalyst for his becoming the *SBCT* rally point topic lead, and he describes the team meeting in Washington D.C. as "a turning point in terms of my growth as a topic lead." Traci and Jay are present at the meeting as well, and attest to the impact it has on their ability and desire to contribute. This understanding leads us to value face-to-face opportunities and to seek out and connect in person with members whenever we travel to different posts.

The relationships that the CC team builds with company commanders who post to the site encourage members to become more actively involved. The team's timely and personal response to a posting on the Web site is the first significant step in relationship building. Through ongoing exchanges, potential topic leads come to understand what CC is all about—they gain a sense of the values and purpose of the team members. This conversation provides a vehicle through which mutual respect, and ultimately a trusting relationship is built.

The CC team is also doing a kind of exploration. They want to know what this company commander's expertise is and what he or she needs that they might be able to provide. They are listening for this person's thinking about the profession. This interaction is perhaps typical of any growing relationship: Both sides are learning about the other in terms of the things that are most important to them.

The desire to have an impact on the profession

In all four stories, we see leaders who want to have an impact, to make things better for their peers and the profession. For example, Rob Mitchell says, "I wanted to make the future of this career field that I love a lot a better place for my successors." These leaders had a desire to make an impact on the profession long before they got involved with CC. They had already started reflecting on their own experiences and had begun sharing their experiences with others. Traci, for example, had written up her experience as an FRG leader to provide continuity for her husband's company. Similarly, Rob Thornton had been sending products to his buddies via email. He says about himself, "In a sense, reflecting is part of the way I work." Being asked by the CC team to take on the topic lead role served as a catalyst for a direction in which each person was already moving; yet being invited by a CC team member to take on that role had significance for them because without the invitation, the person may not have had an outlet for the way in which they wanted to serve the community. CC became a platform from which they could have a greater impact on the profession.

In their communication with members who contribute content, the CC team thanks them and lets them know that their participation is making a difference; however, the positive feedback these leaders receive directly from other leaders in the field—men and women in the arena—is much more meaningful. The importance of feedback from the field is probably stated most clearly in Jay Miseli's story:

> A tank brigade in Korea is going to be better equipped to fight if they're called—wow! I was just floored that a document I wrote had this influence well outside of what I thought of as my relatively small sphere of influence.

Feedback from peers outside the circle of their immediate colleagues gives members a true sense of the impact they are having on the profession. It is thus crucial to design and facilitate professional forums so as to ensure that this feedback occurs.

Availability of Time

Forum members go through periods of time when they are not able to participate as much as they would like. Rob Mitchell notes this phenomenon among the participants in the EOD forum: "Participation fluctuates a lot, sometimes it picks up and sometimes drops off. I think it is a function of how busy we are." Traci Cook recalls, "In September, when my husband changed command, I had more time and I thought, 'I've learned a lot about being an FRG leader,' so I wrote an article and sent it in." Many of the most active team members of CC have been current company commanders whose participation is naturally influenced by their training calendar and deployments.

The whole community is in motion, moving in and out of contributing to the forum as they are able, as well as finding different ways of serving the profession of arms. The leaders of professional forums like CC need to not only accept such movement, but facilitate it—each fluctuation may well represent a new stage of professional development that holds the potential for a new and different way to impact the profession.

Creative license

The phrase "run with it" appears in several of the stories. The storytellers hear this offer from the CC team as a license to be creative: to draw on their own networks, develop their own ideas, and to create something that will be of value to their community. They experience a sense of ownership because they do, in fact, "run with it" and therefore know the impact they are having is of their own making. They feel the pride that comes from knowing that their own ideas and energy are making a difference. This ability to take responsibility for a certain product is also self-reinforcing; people always have the most energy and enthusiasm for something they have built themselves, for something they create.

This sense of ownership requires, on the part of professional forum leaders, a willingness to share control. This is not problematic for the CC team because, through the relationships we build with these members, we are able to know the values, expertise, and intent of those in whom we place this trust. These interactions could be thought of as a screening process, but it is probably more accurate to look at them as cases of mutual attraction. Through the conversations, there emerges a mutual recognition of shared values. The team is able to share control in a way that provides ownership because there are countless company commanders who have this sense of commitment to the profession and who will act on that commitment when the opportunity is provided.

It is not enough for members to have the desire and freedom to take action—they also need the necessary skills and capacity to take action. When Tony asked Rob Mitchell to think through the purpose and vision for the EOD forum, he was helping Rob to be a more effective topic lead. Moreover, part of the team meeting in D.C. was spent teaching leaders how to use the technology platform and to more effectively serve the profession. For example, Rob Thornton learned how to bring himself to the table—to express himself as a topic lead. There is an ongoing pattern of equipping that occurs between the CC team and participating members. Part 2 of this book will focus more on how to equip leaders of a professional forum so that they can effectively run with it!

*****

The four stories that begin this chapter provide insight into the conditions under which members of a community become more actively involved. Once professional forum leaders understand the conditions that move members toward becoming leaders, they can take action to facilitate greater participation.

Key Concepts—Chapter 5

- Engaging in conversation and developing meaningful relationships with members establishes trust and reinforces the desire of members to participate.

- Leaders who become involved in a forum demonstrate through their actions that they already desire to have an impact on the profession. Providing them with a platform to impact the profession and facilitating feedback from the field about the impact they are having further reinforces their commitment.

- Leaders who become actively involved often have an entrepreneurial desire to create. When they are given the license and the capacity to take action, great value is created for the profession.

Chapter 6

Effects-Based Design

...Connecting people, conversation, and content

> Several years ago, an amusing event unfolded at West Point, when the area surrounding Grant Hall was redesigned. After the construction was complete, cadets walking from the Central Area to grab a coffee or to meet a friend at Grant Hall had to walk on the sidewalk ten feet past the door, turn right, and then right again to come back to the door. Or, as they passed the corner of the building, they could cut through the landscaped area and, in three steps, be in the door. This second option was, of course, unacceptable, given that cadets must walk only on approved paths. The lure of the shortcut was a strong one though, and before long there was an obvious trail blazed, making the choice even more enticing.
>
> Cadet leaders, officers, and NCOs responded by "making the correction" whenever they saw someone choosing the easier, wrong way—yet the pattern continued. It became clear that the Commandant of Cadets would have to devote serious resources in order to influence cadets' behavior at this decisive point on the battlefield. One day, two granite stepping-stones appeared in the landscaped area, making it an official pathway, an approved pathway.
>
> Suddenly, there was no longer a problem.

Is there a design component to the problem? The preceding story emphasizes the ongoing relationship between design and human factors. It also demonstrates how a shift in thinking about design can eliminate some problems.

Web site design is a critical part of an effective professional forum, and it is to that subject that we now turn. We call our approach "effects-based design." That is, we design for the specific effect we hope to achieve, which is to connect leaders in conversation about relevant content in a way that advances the practice of command.[1]

Bringing the Conversation Forward

Could vibrant conversation be the defining aspect of a member's experience in the CC online space? We use the metaphor of the "front porch" to capture the effect we want to achieve: friends sitting on the front porch, informally interacting with each other about issues at the core of their command experience, helping each other to learn and to be more effective. Although it is difficult to put a precise number on it, several new discussion posts in the main topics of CC.mil per day create the alive, dynamic, and vibrant experience we are looking to achieve.

Before June 2004, this objective—vibrant "front porch" conversation—was not being achieved. Conversation was not central in a CC member's experience. Asking ourselves whether there was a design component to this problem revealed some underlying problems: We discovered that most members were not aware that each topic on the site had its own discussion area. And, those members who did know found it frustrating to have to click through all the topics to view the discussions. Instead of a vibrant front-porch conversation, what we had was more like a collection of empty meeting rooms.

So, our assessment was that design was a part of the problem. We then designed to achieve the desired effect, implementing several changes on 5 June 2004.

One of the most significant changes implemented was to collate recent discussion comments posted throughout the online space in a "recent discussions" box on the front page of CC.mil:

---

[1] Effects-based design is a way of thinking that has application beyond the Web site for our team, e.g., designing face-to-face workshops to include conversations and group interactions. However, in this chapter we focus specifically on the online aspect of the CC professional forum.

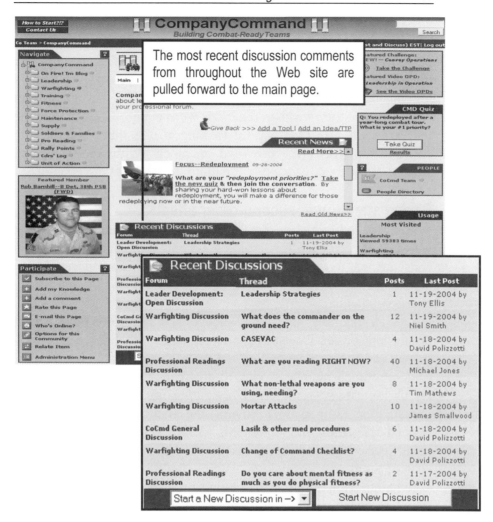

Thus, a question like Tony Ellis' posted in the *Leader Development* topic, which might have gone unnoticed before the design change, now gets immediate front-page visibility.

The recent discussions area is designed so that members can easily see which topic the discussion is in, the title of the discussion thread, number of posts in the thread, and date and name of the last person to post. As a result, it's much easier for members to follow and to join in the ongoing conversations.

This design change applies to all topics on the Web site, meaning that topic leads can choose to have recent discussion comments from any topic they designate collated and featured front-and-center on their topic pages as well.

After we made this design change, we noticed an immediate increase in discussion comments. From May 2004—the month prior to the change—to August, the number of comments per month increased 300%. Prior to this design change, members logging on to CompanyCommand.army.mil, like the West Point cadets in the story we shared earlier, were being forced to take the long way around. One way of looking at it is that "bringing the conversation forward" provided members with the stepping-stones. Now, they have a direct path to the current conversation.

Paying attention to second-order effects

With every individual design change, there have been impacts that we were not prepared for—some good and some bad. Unintended consequences go with the territory. It is therefore necessary to heighten awareness following a design change and to continually assess what is happening.

As an example, one consequence of having the most recent discussions pulled forward to the main page was that we, in effect, trained members to depend on the main page to track discussions. This reinforced members' lack of awareness of the different topic discussion areas such as *Warfighting* and *Leadership*. As participation ramped up following the change in June 2004, we noticed questions and comments—some very important ones—being pushed off the recent discussion list on the main page and "out of sight" very quickly. For example, one member in Iraq asked a question about air-to-ground fires coordination. It was an excellent question that had the potential to spark a productive and needed conversation. It was also the type of question that most people want to think about before answering. Within two days of the question being posted, it was no longer visible on the main page and, despite the fact that it still existed in the *Warfighting* topic discussion area, for most members, it was gone. This means that members who might have answered the question after they thought about it for a few days could not because they didn't know where the question was.

For our team, this experience further clarified the importance of topic leads and facilitators. As a result of this experience, topic leads are more tuned-in to the discussion comments that are generated in their topics and track them—sometimes replying to a question that drops off the main page to "bring it forward again."

This is an example of a desired effect—greater participation in discussions—being achieved, and yet that very success creating unforeseen conditions that require further action. Heightening awareness following design changes allows for an appropriate response to second-order effects as they emerge.

Facilitating Connections, Fostering A Sense of Community

At the same time that we were thinking through "bringing the conversation forward," we were also looking at ways to create more connections between members and to foster a sense of professional community—two things that we believe are critical in a professional forum. We mentioned the image of a front-porch conversation, and part of this is a sense of social presence—the feeling that you are on the front porch *with* other members of the profession rather than in an electronic library all alone.

One way to increase connections and a sense of professional community is to give members visibility of each other. We therefore changed the design so that when a member logs in, his or her name automatically appears in a "People Online" box that is displayed on every topic in the online space. Moreover, the members' names are hyperlinked to their "dog tags" or member profiles. Thus, members get an immediate sense that

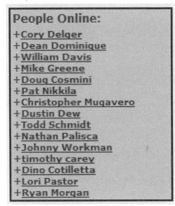

there are other people "in the space" with them, and they can click on the names to find out who they are. Member dog tags not only provide a wealth of information about the person, including the key experiences that they bring to the table, but they also provide links to comments or knowledge that the person has submitted as well as connections to other members that have visited the dog tag. Thus, by making logged-in members visible, designers create the possibility for connections to people as well as to content. As one example, if you were to click on **"Ryan Morgan"** in the above example list of "People Online," you would discover that he recently gave up command of HHC/2-502 IN, his second company in the 101ˢᵗ Infantry Division, and that he is currently working in the TRADOC futures center. Knowing that he spent a full year in Iraq, along with the other experiences listed, provides context about who he is and what knowledge he has to offer.

Ryan Morgan
Morgan, Ryan [Personal Topic]

Date Added: *01-15-2004*
Date Modified: *08-23-2004*

Ryan Morgan [Export Vcard for Outlook]
Past Company Commander
C-2-502 IN RGT, HHC-2-502 IN RGT
Infantry

Email them at: ryan.morgan@us.army.mil

> Add this person to the contact list on your Dog Tag <

Current Organization:
HQ, TRADOC, Futures center

Current Position:
GO's XO, TRADOC, Futures center

Current Post:
Ft. Monroe, Va

About Me:
1997-2000 - 1-8 IN RGT (M), Ft. Carson, CO: Bradley PL, MTR PL, CO XO

Key experiences I have had:
Conducted M2 BFV-ODS Feilding C-1-8 IN (M)

Partisipated in hosting elements of the Royal Irish Regement while with 2-502 IN

Operation Iraqi Fredom 1 (12 mos)

What I love about leading soldiers:
Their inteligence and ingenuity. Their ability to adapt and overcome any situation.

Favorite Saying:
its a great day to be a soldier

Moreover, when you scroll further down Ryan's dog tag, you find the most recent discussions that Ryan has participated in, to include hyperlinks to each:

Latest Discussion Posts Ryan has made:

Knowledge Ryan Morgan is related to:
20 conversation posts. Most recent:

"Introduce Yourself!" (16 replies) [CompanyCommand]

"Taking Command In Country" (4 replies) [CompanyCommand]

"Body Armor" (7 replies) [CompanyCommand]

"MFO Sanai advice, recommendations, lessons learned" (4 replies)

"Best Book for Leaders in Iraq to read?" (8 replies) [Co Team]

If you click on the first one—"Introduce Yourself!"—you see that Ryan introduced himself in the *HQ Commander* rally point, and that he has made himself available to other HQ commanders, writing:

> Prior to taking HHC, I commanded C-2-502 IN for 16 months including during OIF. Before that, I was a BDE plans officer for 2 Bde, 101st ABN (AASLT). I took troops from train-up and deployment through combat and SASO, and finally redeployment and reintegration. I would be happy to be able to help anyone as best I can.

And, in the process of reading this comment in the "Introduce Yourself" discussion thread, you see other discussion posts. For example, the next one after Ryan's is by David Polizzotti, who writes:

> I'm currently in the process of recovering from OIF and starting to develop training plans for my Scouts, Mortars, and Medics, which have been decimated by PCS turbulence. I'm interested to see what advice there is out there for prepping training ideas for these platoons.

As with all discussion comments on the site, David's name and picture are embedded with his comment, and they are hyperlinked to his dog tag. A click on Ryan Morgan's name has led you to David:

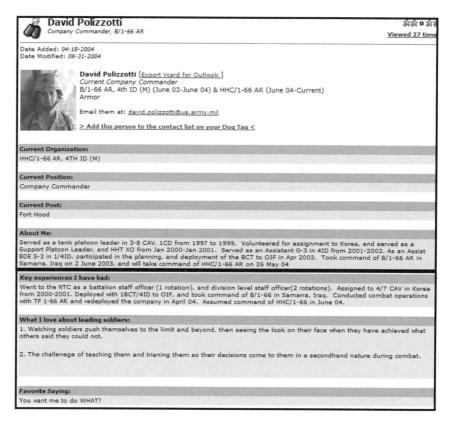

As a result of the "People Online" feature, members are gaining a sense of each other's presence—and in the process, they are connecting with other members and content. We especially like this example because it is precisely how *we* connected with David Polizzotti! We like to call this *intentional serendipity* in that this type of design creates the conditions for accidental, valuable connections to flourish. Our experience with professional forums like CC that are tightly focused on a specific practice is that more paths to people and content equal more value-adding connections.

A second way that we sought to reinforce a sense of professional community and to foster connections was by featuring members on the main page with a picture and, again, linking the person's name to their dog tag. Thus, when you click on **"Pat Nikkila,"** his dog tag opens:

Featured Member
Pat Nikkila (759th EOD)

 Pat Nikkila
Nikkila, Pat [Personal Topic]

Date Added: *05-22-2003*
Date Modified: *08-25-2004*

 **Pat Nikkila**
Past Company Commander
759th EOD
Ordnance

Email them a

In the "About Me" portion of the featured member's dog tag, we describe why we are featuring him or her, and try to include something personal. In this case, we created a mini interview:

Featured CC Member: Pat Nikkila is a featured CC member during the week of 22 August 2004. Pat has been nominated by Rob Mitchell and the EOD Rally Point for his exceptional leadership during OIF 1 as well as his phenomenal commitment to the profession and the EOD community.

CC: When was this picture taken?

Pat: It was taken on Day 7 of the initial ground war in Iraq. We were attached to the 3d Infantry Division and stayed in Iraq until OCT 03. We were about 12 kilometers west of Najaf during that incident (we were cleaning up unexploded ordnance).

CC: Is there anything you would like to pass on to current and future Company Commanders?

Pat: The only nugget I can share is "Learn the Lessons Learned." You have to be a student of your profession and there are plenty of resources out there -- from your chain of command to other resources such as the AKO knowledge center and this Company Command forum that offer insight and experience. If you happen to come across a situation where there is little documentation or resources that you can pull from, after you're complete with the operation - WRITE IT DOWN and give it to your chain of command--AND SHARE IT WITH THE PROFESSION IN FORUMS LIKE THIS! Unfortunately, many good lessons learned are not shared or documented and therefore are...never learned.

The CC professional forum *is* company commanders—present, future, and past. Showcasing pictures of members puts a face on the profession and makes members' online experience a personal one. When you combine this technique with the visibility of the members who are in the space or on the front porch with you right now ("People Online") and the most recent discussion comments, members have an experience that they want to return to.

Making Content More Visible

Having high-quality, relevant content is incredibly important to a professional forum. Content attracts members (by providing them immediate value), connects members (by bringing together those who contribute content with those who use it), shapes members' conversations (by setting the tone and reinforcing the purpose of the forum), and motivates members (by enabling them to contribute directly to their profession's base of knowledge). However, even the best content is useless unless members know about it.

There are many ways to increase awareness of content in an online professional forum, some of which you saw in the previous discussion of "dog tags," which include hyperlinks to the person's content contributions. Now, we will focus on organizing content, the "search" function, and topic-lead actions to feature content.

The topic-based organization of the CC online space is one way that we have designed to increase awareness of content. By breaking the space into the main topics of command, e.g., *Leadership*, *Warfighting*, *Training*, etc. members are already becoming aware of the breadth of content available. Topics can be further broken down to facilitate organization of content. We have all had the experience of discovering a useful book while browsing through a bookstore or library, and this same thing happens when you organize content in a professional forum by topic. Members find relevant content simply by going to the topic they are interested in—another example of intentional serendipity.

A second way that members find the content they need is through the search function. We won't say much about it here because it is one feature that needs some serious improvement in the CC forum; the good news is that Tomoye, Inc.—the company we are partnered with—is developing a much-improved solution and we look forward to unveiling it in the next year.

Finally, topic leads can take action to generate awareness of content within their topics much as magazine or newspaper editors do. Mark Derber, for example, uses both the "free text" area at the top of the Leadership topic and the "featured content" area on the right side to highlight and draw attention to content:[2]

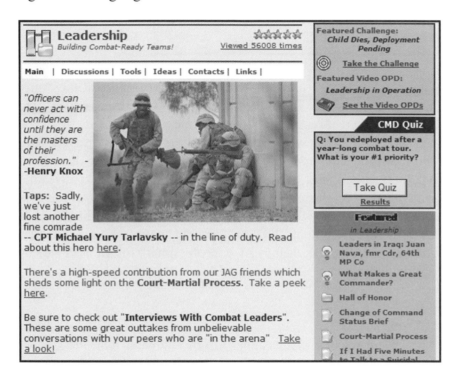

With similar effect, the *Warfighting* team uses announcements to draw attention to new content on the *Afghan Commander* topic:

---

[2] Notice also how Mark Derber creates context and establishes the tone with a picture and quotation. The tagline *Building Combat-Ready Teams!* is found on every topic within the CC forum, reinforcing the purpose throughout the forum.

Each underlined item is hyperlinked to the content it describes. In the case of names, the link is to their dog tags.

These last examples are topic-lead driven, meaning that they only happen when a topic lead takes action. Even with proactive topic leads, however, it remains difficult for members to be aware of the constant flow of new content. Based on our experience with "bringing the conversation forward" to a most recent discussion box on the main page, we envision a design change that creates the same effect for content. In other words, when new content is uploaded anywhere within CC, it is also automatically displayed in a "most recent content" box on the main page. This realization underscores that the design of a professional forum is a never-ending process.

*****

The impact of a professional forum is greater than the sum of its parts, and it is therefore critical that designers "see the whole" even as they seek to improve individual aspects of the forum. It is helpful here to compare an effective professional forum with an effective Army unit. An effective unit is a complex mix of many things—for example, leadership, training, discipline, physical fitness, and morale. Although we label them in order to assess and improve them, we are keenly aware that they are interwoven and inseparable. For example, leadership is evident in effective physical training; and, physically fit Soldiers lead more effectively.

With CC, we have found that conversation, content, connections, and a sense of professional community all work together to create an effective professional forum. To be deficient in any one of them is to be less effective overall. Web site designers reinforce the success of a professional forum when they design to achieve effects in these critical areas.

Key Concepts—Chapter 6

- Asking "Is there a design component to the problem?" can be incredibly helpful when it comes to Web site design.

- Small design changes can have a significant impact.

- Effects-based design focuses professional forum leaders on achieving effects in those areas that are most important to a professional forum. For example,
  - Vibrant, front-porch conversation (Bringing the conversation forward),
  - Facilitating connections between members,
  - Fostering a sense of professional community, and
  - Increasing awareness of content.

- Finally, professional forum design is a continuous and iterative process. Assessment must be continuous as solutions lead to both the desired effects and unexpected second-order effects.

PART 2

In Part 1, you read stories of a professional forum in action: leaders connecting in conversation to improve their effectiveness and advance the practice of company command.

Part 2 is the "how to" section of the book. It focuses on the practical activities of professional-forum leadership: first steps, growing a team, and putting the key elements of connections, conversation, and content into action. Part 2 closes with a description of the Afghan Commander Prep Initiative, an event that brings together many of the principles and techniques presented throughout the book.

Chapter 7

First Steps for Forum Leaders

What follows is a conversation between a CC leader and an MP company commander who is an active CC member and wants to become more involved. We will call her Deborah. She is a composite of many people and the conversation is based on hundreds of interactions that our team has had over the last four years.

> ***Deborah:*** *I can't tell you how much I've gained from being part of CC, especially with the Iraq deployment. Now that I'm more experienced...well, I feel like I'm in a position to give back. How can I get more involved?*
>
> **CC Leader:** Well, you are already making a difference every time you join in a discussion or send in something you're learning. As far as getting more involved, there are lots of ways: Contribute to the *Cdrs' Log*, become a command contact or a topic lead—the sky is the limit. I think the key is to understand your unique experience and what you're passionate about, and then we can unleash you in service of COs. Some commanders are total studs on maintenance; others are fanatics about training—they live for it! Is there a topic that really "jazzes you up" as a company commander? Is there some area that you have a lot of experience in and that you feel driven to share with others about?
>
> ***Deborah:*** *The first thing that comes to mind for me is convoy ops—we did some serious driving in Iraq and boy is that topic important...and, well, I've had three 1SGs—the cdr/1SG relationship is something I think is critical.*
>
> *Conversation continued on next page...*

CC Leader: Hey, no rush...why don't you take a look around the online space and see what connects with you the most. We do have some specific needs, but the real deal is that we want to get you involved in an area that you care deeply about.

Deborah: You mentioned needs. What's an example of a need?

CC Leader: Well, several current topic leads are transitioning this summer and could sure use some help. The *Training* topic is one example. We're also looking for someone to head up a new section specifically focused on company command AARs. The AAR you submitted from Iraq is *really* good, so that new area might be right up your alley. Also, a lot of MP officers have been joining CC, and we don't have an MP rally point yet. With your recent experience commanding in Iraq, you might be the perfect person to start that up.

[Several weeks pass.]

Deborah: Sorry for the delay in getting back to you. Redeployment issues, family, you know the deal. I went through the different areas of the site, but I kept coming back to the idea of starting an MP rally point—a space specifically for us to connect and share ideas and lessons learned. That would be cool.

CC Leader: Yes! Five MP officers have joined CC in the last 24hrs alone—three of them are in Iraq right now, either in command or getting ready to take command. I'll send you their dog tags (member profiles) so that you can connect with them and let them know about their new rally point! You are going to make a huge impact.

Deborah: So, how do I get started? What do I do?

Note: We will continue to use Deborah and the MP rally point as an example throughout Part 2, indicating so with an MP rally point symbol in the margin.

This chapter answers Deborah's question—"Ok, so how do I get started?"—and it focuses leaders on the important first steps of professional-forum leadership: setting direction, building a team, and creating an organizing framework.

Setting Direction

The process of setting direction is an essential "first step" in moving toward the kind of professional forum you are seeking to create—setting direction provides the azimuth. Three practices that have helped our team set direction for the projects we initiate include defining a clear purpose, envisioning the future, and clarifying core values.

> **First Steps For Forum Leaders**
>
> ➤ **Setting Direction**
>
>   1. **Defining a clear purpose**
>
>   2. **Envisioning the future**
>
>   3. **Clarifying core values**
>
>   • Building A Team
>
>   • Organizing the Online Space

1. Defining a clear purpose

Purpose unleashes and energizes professional-forum leaders toward effective action. Our strategies, how we invest our time and resources, the people involved, the projects we initiate, and our daily decisions—what we say "yes" or "no" to—all flow from purpose. The sharper the purpose, the more valuable the experience that CC can create. There are two questions that have helped us hone our purpose:

- *Why do we exist?*

- *Whom are we serving?*

An analogy that has helped our team focus as we answered these two questions is that of light shining on a wall (the Army). Professional-forum leaders can weakly illuminate the whole wall, or they can focus their energy like a laser beam that powerfully illuminates one part of the wall. We choose to concentrate our efforts and resources and, in so doing, deliver powerful results in service of company commanders. The following description of why we exist and whom we are serving guides our team:

We exist to advance the practice of company command.
We are focused on serving company commanders.

The second question, "Whom are we serving?" was not an obvious question for our team initially; however, we have found that answering it creates essential insight and completes the first question that gets at why we exist. *Who* is in the conversation has a significant impact *on* the conversation. People understand this intuitively when it comes to face-to-face conversations. For example, with a group of peer company commanders, you might feel comfortable asking for help and soliciting input on a leadership dilemma you are wrestling with. This is also true in a professional forum, and it is why we are mindful of membership and who has access to the forum. If you imagine CC as a gathering of professionals around a HMMWV hood talking about the things that matter most when it comes to company command, you can see how who is in the conversation changes the nature of the conversation. Our experience has been that when members see that the great majority of participants are people on the same road with them—company commanders—they are much more likely to participate.

 So, if we were in a conversation with Deborah, our new topic lead, we would talk about the purpose of CC and ask her to think about and articulate the purpose of the MP rally point. We would invite her to treat this as an ongoing process—a conversation she returns to regularly and one she invites her new team members to participate in. Here is one possibility for the MP rally point purpose:

We are present, future, and past commanders who
come together to collectively improve MP company
commander effectiveness.[1]

There is a natural tendency for a professional forum to drift, unintentionally, beyond the scope of its purpose. A vinedresser (think grapes) will tell you that disciplined pruning leads to healthy vines that bear quality fruit. Untended grape plants look very

---

[1] This process also applies to topics such as *Training*, which supports the overall CC purpose with a focus specifically on improving company commander effectiveness in the area of training.

impressive yet produce lackluster results. Experienced vine dressers cut away unnecessary growth with their eye on the harvest. Similarly, we seek to steadfastly focus on our purpose—improving company commander effectiveness—and we are ever ready to cut away those things that do not serve that purpose—to say "no" to good in order to say "yes" to great.

2. Envisioning the future

Vision can be defined as a "picture of the future we seek to create."[2] A simple exercise that has sparked valuable insights for our team is,

> *If _____ were happening, it would be a '10' on a scale of '1-10' and I would be absolutely inspired.*

Fill in the blank with a vivid description of what you would love to see happen, what a great future would look like. This process is especially effective when it is a team event in which a powerful *shared* image of the future is created.

When you articulate a vision of what great would be like, and you compare that with an honest assessment of the way things really are (current reality), you have what Peter Senge calls creative tension. He uses the image of two hands pulling a rubber band apart to communicate this concept. The tension is positive because it energizes and mobilizes people to move current reality toward the envisioned future they desire.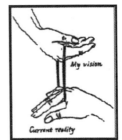

The alternative—relaxing the vision in order to resolve the tension—is a path to mediocrity. Sometimes, however, limitations such as resources or technology prevent you from moving as fast as you would like. The key in those situations is not to relax the creative tension—to maintain the image of the future—so that when something changes (technology, for example), you see it and take advantage of it. Your greatest breakthroughs will occur when

---

[2] Peter Senge, "The Practice of Innovation," *Leader to Leader Journal,* Summer 1998: p. 5 (http://www.pfdf.org/leaderbooks/l2l/summer98/senge.html). A must read! Also, read Jim Collins, "Aligning Action with Values" found at: http://leadertoleader.org/leaderbooks/l2l/summer96/collins.html.

you refuse to relax the vision; over time, a shared, compelling vision draws current reality toward it.

3. Clarifying core values

Core values describe who you are and what you think is important. They influence the way you act on a day-to-day basis. A question to ask yourself as you unearth or clarify your core values is,

> *How will we act as we move along the azimuth we have set for ourselves?*

Early in the development of CC, our team spent considerable time talking about what we were seeking to create together. In what turned into an ongoing conversation, we clarified our purpose and core values. We were less concerned about identifying what purpose and values we thought would "work," and more concerned about unearthing what was core to us personally. The values we identified serve as a beacon that guides our behavior as we seek to accomplish the purpose we have committed ourselves to.

CC Team Values

Positive voice with a focus on solutions. CC is positive and practical—focused like a laser beam on the practice of company command and those things that are important to company commanders.

Passion for quality. We seek excellence in all that we do. We choose quality over quantity, and we are continuously improving and forward looking. Company commanders are compelled to participate because of the value that the experience creates for them. Members take pride in the quality of the forum as well as in knowing that the team is constantly pushing to make it better.

Innovative and creative. We challenge our assumptions, take risks, and are constantly learning in order to achieve breakthroughs that will serve company commanders. If we aren't on the cutting edge, we are working to get there.

Committed to the Army. We love the Army and its Soldiers. We live out the Army values, and we are dedicated stewards of the profession. We find great satisfaction in knowing that our work directly serves the strategic goals and vision of the Army.

Grass Roots. CC *is* company commanders—present, future, and past. It is by the profession, for the profession.

Building A Team

In a five-year study of organizations that went from being good to being great, Jim Collins discovered a clear trend: the organizations that became great focused first on bringing the right people together—building the team. Collins writes,

> The right people don't need to be tightly managed or fired up; they will be self-motivated by the inner drive to produce the best results and to be part of creating something great. If you have the wrong people, it doesn't matter whether you discover the right direction; you still won't have a great company. Great vision without great people is irrelevant.[3]

Although Collins is adamant about getting the "right people on the bus first," we have also found that the right people are drawn to a worthwhile purpose and vision of the future. Like the chicken or the egg question, purpose and people are both essential for great things to emerge and the two are reinforcing.

What follows is a description of four ideas that will help you think in practical terms about building a team.

First Steps For Forum Leaders

✓ Setting Direction

➤ **Building A Team**
  1. Creating an initial core team
  2. Activating your pointmen
  3. Recruiting command contacts
  4. Making the team a team

• Organizing the Online Space

---

1. Creating an initial core team

Two questions to ask yourself as you begin thinking about building a team are:

- *Who would I love to work with on this?*

- *Who has already demonstrated by their actions a desire to share knowledge and to serve others?*

---

[3] Jim Collins, *Good to Great*, 2001: p. 42.

Invite these people to join you. Our experience has been that when two or three like-hearted leaders are intertwined, they become a triple-braided rope—strong as steel. Two or three people create better ideas, energize each other, carry the load when one person is out of the net, and otherwise spur each other on.

If *THEY* Build It, *THEY* Will Come

Many organizations take the "If *WE* build it, *THEY* will come" approach. This approach is usually followed by "make them come" and "it didn't work."

Our approach is, "If *company commanders* build it, *company commanders* will come." Professional forums must be designed and facilitated by people who are experienced in and passionate about the particular practice they are seeking to serve. They will intuitively understand what is relevant and valuable to the practice. Moreover, *who they know* and their reputation in the practice is absolutely priceless and will directly influence their ability to build a team.

---

2. Activating your pointmen

As you lay the groundwork for your launch, you will want to get the word out to your potential members and contributors and ask for input from them.[4] In simplest terms, the pointman concept entails reaching many through a few. Applying this concept, Deborah and her team would begin talking with the people that they know in the MP community and would ask them to spread the word and to participate in the forum.[5] Think of this as a grassroots marketing and content-building plan.

---

[4] The principles that apply to launching a new topic or professional forum also apply to launching an important discussion thread—something we call a *priority* conversation. Moreover, leaders who want to reinvigorate an existing topic can also apply these same pointman principles.

[5] The CompanyCommand.army.mil member database is another resource available to topic leads. Searching by type of unit, for example, Deborah and team can quickly connect to the MP officers who are CC members.

In order to identify pointmen, Deborah and her core team might ask themselves a series of questions like:

- *Who are the MP company commanders— current as well as past and future? (and, Where are they located?)*
- *Who do we already have relationships with?*
- *Who do we need to develop relationships with?*

Drawing what we call a network map (NETMAP) can help Deborah and her team to visualize the MP community—to see relationships they already have with MP officers as well as relationships that they need to initiate:

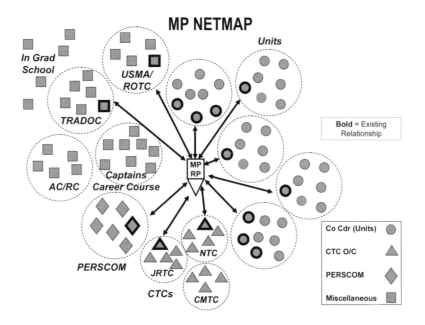

There are sophisticated network mapping techniques available,[6] but even a basic picture on a dry erase board of who is connected to whom can be extremely helpful. In the NETMAP shown above, Deborah and her team mapped out where all present, future, and past MP commanders were located. Each symbol represents a person, and the bolded ones are people with whom the team has a

---

[6] See Appendix 2, "From Our Bookshelf," to find several books about the value of people networks as well as techniques to visualize and reinforce them.

relationship. Deborah and her team are primarily focused on connecting with current company commanders; however, they also know that past commanders are an extremely valuable source of experience and are often in a position that allows them to give back to the community. Additionally, some past commanders have expertise and social connections based on where they work. For example, Deborah is good friends with an MP observer controller (O/C) at the National Training Center (NTC). This person can connect the team to other O/Cs as well as to the MP commanders who rotate through the training center. Because of their company command experience and the number of MP officers that they are constantly in contact with, officers in roles like O/Cs, PERSCOM branch managers, and small group instructors (SGIs) are key nodes in the network.

In the example MP NETMAP, you will notice that there is no arrow to the MP captain's career course (CCC), meaning that the team doesn't have an existing connection with any of the SGIs there. Considering that MP SGIs are all experienced MP company commanders and every future MP commander goes through the MP CCC, initiating a relationship with an SGI could be very important.

Identifying and connecting with pointmen is the first part of this process. Subsequently, Deborah informs them about what she is doing and enlists their support. Next, she solicits content from them to populate the topic or forum. *Once the conditions are set*, she sends them a launch announcement that they can forward to all of the MP officers they know. Here is an example of a potential email announcing the launch of the MP rally point:

Email from Deborah to MP Team re Launch MP Rally Point

MP Team:

We are ready to LAUNCH, LAUNCH, LAUNCH the *MP Rally Point*! **Please forward this note to *every* MP company commander you know—past, present, and future.** Together, we are going to create a phenomenal gathering place within the CompanyCommand forum to connect and talk about the things that matter to MP commanders.

If you have not registered via http://CompanyCommand.army.mil, please do and then find our space in the *Rally Point* section. To get things started, please "introduce yourself" in the forum and check out several discussions already going strong on topics like convoy ops, redeployment, and the cdr/1SG relationship.

Our first focus area is going to be combat-leader interviews. If you have experience commanding in combat, we need you to complete a simple web-based interview that you can link to via our rally point (we've got two already completed and posted). Imagine the impact if we all stepped up to the plate and did this one thing. Sharing what we are learning with each other isn't just a good idea any more—it is a must!

Three ways you can contribute right away: 1. Introduce yourself in the rally point. 2. Send in one tool or idea that is making a difference for you as a CO. 3. Forward this email to every MP CO you know.

We look forward to hanging out with you in the rally point and—together—becoming better commanders!

The pointman concept entails leaders leveraging their current relationships and continuously developing new relationships so that they can effectively communicate with those who would both benefit from and add value to the forum. It is a grass-roots mechanism to get connected.[7]

---

[7] As described in the introduction to this book, "pointman" is a term we also use to describe members who step up to perform critical missions in a wider sense than getting the word out and setting the conditions for a launch. For example, we would call Paul Huszar, who designed the CC coin and did the leg work in Korea for producing it, a pointman; Rob McCormick was the pointman for a *Command Challenge* scenario; and Tom Woodie was the pointman for company commander seminars with captains attending CAS3.

Paul Revere's Pointman Concept

In his book *The Tipping Point*, Malcolm Gladwell tells the story of Paul Revere and the word-of-mouth epidemic he started in order to warn the colonists that *"The British are coming!"* What you probably didn't know is that another patriot and friend of Revere— William Dawes—set out on horseback that same night from the same starting point and traveled a different route. Dawes carried the same news and was just as dedicated as Revere, but he was terribly ineffective at getting the word out.

According to Gladwell, "So few men from one town— Waltham—fought the following day that some subsequent historians concluded that it must have been a strongly pro-British community. It wasn't. The people of Waltham just didn't find out the British were coming until it was too late."

Revere was insatiably social, and he had friends and acquaintances across the region. During his mad midnight ride, he knew who to connect with and he leveraged his relationships. Dawes, on the other hand, just gave the news to the first person he could find. He didn't have the relationships like Revere, and he had to rely solely on the importance of the message to convince people to take action. You can picture the confusion in the middle of the night and, through a social network lens, Dawes' lack of success is understandable.

Two centuries later, the principles at work in this story still apply. Although he had to ride a horse to make it happen, Revere used the pointman concept we've described—through a few key people, he reached thousands and, in the process, changed history.

3. Recruiting command contacts

Command contacts are members who have a depth of experience in a topic and have volunteered to make themselves available to company commanders. Command contacts respond to questions that members ask online, identify knowledge gaps for their topic, and do much of the work of connecting members. The command contacts along with their respective topic lead(s) are thought leaders for that topic.

Email from a CC Leader to CC Team re Command Contacts

Team: The command contact concept may, over time, become the most important factor in our ability to deliver awesome value to current and future company commanders. Think about the most squared-away company commanders that you have seen, and then recruit them to be contacts—in the process, you are growing your team! Most officers who are passionate about command are eager to make a difference by being available for current and future commanders—we just need to ask them. Is there a CC member that is especially active in your topic? He would probably love to be a contact! As you grow your team, you create value for company commanders and you give more people the opportunity to make a difference.

There seem to be three main ways that command contacts emerge:

- Many command contacts emerge out of the initial pointman process.
- Some contacts are recruited by topic leads based on their expertise or set of experiences in a particular topic. The topic lead might know them personally, or they may simply have observed their participation online or via their dog tag experience description.
- And members also take the initiative and email topic leads directly to let them know that they would like to take on that role.

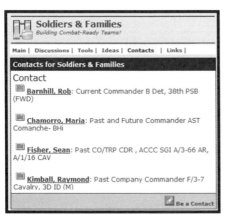

CompanyCommand.army.mil is designed so that command contacts are displayed within their respective topics. This example shows how the command contacts in the *Soldiers & Families* topic are displayed. Clicking on a name opens the person's dog tag.

Thus, members gain awareness of and have a way to easily connect with experienced leaders who have the desire to make a difference—to be contacted.

This next email is Ray Kimball responding to a member who volunteered to become a command contact. It is an excellent example of a topic lead clarifying what is expected of a command contact.

Email from Topic Lead Ray Kimball to *Personnel* Contact

Thanks for your desire to serve company commanders. By volunteering to become a command contact for the *Personnel* topic, you are making yourself available to current and future company-level commanders. Officers will be able to tap into your experience, ask you questions, and otherwise seek your input. The more information you provide on your dog tag, the better, especially about the subject of personnel. We have found that the more specific you are in describing your experience and what you are available to help current and future commanders with, the more likely it will be that people will contact you for help when they need it.

In addition, we would appreciate your help building content on the *Personnel* topic page by contributing tools, ideas, etc., that have made a difference for you. Finally, as a *Personnel* contact, please subscribe to that topic and regularly check and contribute as you can to the conversations there.

---

4. Making the team a team

When a group of like-hearted leaders come together around a clear and worthwhile purpose, amazing things are possible; however, for a group to become a cohesive team—and attain its full potential—professional-forum leaders have to be intentional about the practice of *team building*. Our experience has been that doing the work of a professional forum *together* and seeing the positive impact of the work significantly affects whether a group becomes a cohesive team. Additionally, it is important that team members are equipped and given the license to create. In other words, they must have the skills necessary to do the work and freedom of action to carry it out in the manner and timing that they see is most effective.[8] If team members believe in the purpose, have trust in the people they are working with, and know that they are an important part of "making it happen," their personal commitment will be high.

---

[8] These ideas are themes in Chapter 5, "Finding the Heart of the Profession."

Two practices that reinforce this sense of purpose, trust, and awareness of personal impact are: communication and building camaraderie. What follows is a menu of ideas that will serve to spark your own thinking about how to effectively communicate with team members and build team camaraderie.

Communicating with the team. It has been said that 90% of an effective relationship is communication. The #1 point here is for professional-forum leaders to be intentional about keeping their team informed about what is happening—to stay connected using email, mail, phone calls, and face-to-face conversations. Balance this with your team's availability; in other words, don't overwhelm them. One thing that you will want to routinely update is your team's contact information—to include phone number, mailing address, and email. Create an email distribution (distro) list of the team and establish a "commo battle rhythm." For example, a topic lead might have a distro list with her command contacts, pointmen, and other active members that she emails once a month with a description of what is happening in the topic, specific ways they can help, and a story or positive feedback comment that a member sent in. Some additional suggestions:

- Encourage team members who are located at the same post to gather once a month to discuss specific aspects of the team's work.

- Mail hand-written notes to team members. Print up their dog tag (member profile) and write the note directly on it. Doing so creates another connection between the virtual and the physical world, and reinforces their membership.

- Conduct a "live huddle" online (chat) focused on a specific aspect of the forum.

- Send out a team newsletter.

- Create a space online specifically for the team. For example, within CompanyCommand.army.mil, we established what we call the *On Fire! Team Blog*. In this space we share ideas, ask questions, and keep each other up-to-date about what is happening. In one ongoing discussion thread we capture positive feedback we receive from members so that everyone on the CC team sees it. Another serves as a tutorial that new team members can access to learn how to do basic tasks such as featuring and editing content in the forum.

Effective communication goes beyond simply emailing team members. What is said and how it is said is important as well. In order to understand this, we recently studied topic leads' communication with team members (and prospective team members). Although we didn't find a recipe for communication, we did unearth several consistent themes in both the way they communicated—a positive, inspirational tone—and the content of their communication. We have taken our observations of topic leads' communication and turned it into a list of five communication tips for professional-forum leaders:

Commo Tips for Professional-Forum Leaders

1. Continually share purpose. Reinforce why the professional forum exists and whom the team is serving.

2. Specifically communicate the impact that the team or the person is having, and thank them for it. Without feedback, people may be unaware of the value they are providing, the difference they are making.

3. Pass on a tip or lesson learned that will help them be more effective in their work with the forum. This could be a specific tip about how to use the technology platform (e.g., hyperlink text) or a lesson you recently learned. This is most effective when it is prompted by something the team member is working on right now (i.e., a "just in time" tip that ties in to their current activity).

4. If the person doesn't have something specific to do for the team, get them engaged. Describe what that person can do—something that will make a real and practical difference—and ask them to do it.

5. Convey a genuine interest in the person as a person, beyond just their work with the team.

In order to bring these principles alive, we will share a quick example. After a brand new topic lead posted a note in an online discussion, an experienced CC team member wrote him and gave him the following feedback. Read the email and then assess it against the "Commo Tips" above and think about how it might apply to you.

Email from Experienced CC Team Leader to New Topic Lead

I think you are a born topic lead my brother. One example is your note back on the Soldier dying/educational IRA idea. You engaged with Art, you mentioned another piece of content to let people know about relevant content that they might not otherwise see, and you asked others to share their own ideas on the subject. It just doesn't get any better than that.

Training Tip: *Create hyperlinked text.* You can highlight a word and then click on the icon of the globe (top, right side when typing a message or knowledge object), and then paste the url in. For example, you could hyperlink the article you mentioned so that when people click on it, they go straight to the article.

The subject of how to deal with a Soldier dying in your unit is probably one we need to bring to the top, so I am very interested in seeing if your note gets any response.

Rock on! It sure is awesome having you onboard.

Building Camaraderie. Effective teams are cohesive and committed to a common cause. They draw energy and inspiration from a shared sense of team identity and collective commitment. There is no formula for creating teamwork. However, there are ways that professional-forum leaders can develop camaraderie. A few ideas that have been meaningful to our team in this area include:

- Refer to members as a team: All of our leaders are included in the term the CC team—including pointmen, command contacts, topic leads, and the support team.

- Use gear—such as team hats, pens, and coins—to communicate membership and being a part of something really cool, significant, and of exceptional quality. While some might consider these items as "nice to have," we consider them mission essential to building camaraderie amongst a team of dedicated volunteers.

- Give awards to acknowledge exceptional contributions to the profession. For example, we give team members the "Heavy Hitter Award" (a bat with the person's name and the CompanyCommand logo engraved) as a small token of the profession's appreciation for their service.

- Take the *Pro-Reading Challenge* together as a team (see Chapter 3, "Talking About Books"). For example, we bought *The Tipping Point,* by Malcolm Gladwell for the entire CC team and engaged in a discussion about the book in the *On Fire! Team Blog.*

- Know what people have going on and make a personal difference for each other. Do this, for example, by connecting team members who are at the same post, writing letters of recommendation for team members, and knowing when they are facing a significant deployment or other life event.

- Perhaps the most powerful team-building event we have been able to pull off was a face-to-face gathering in Washington D.C. in January 2004. We brought together 21 team members for three days and called it the "On Fire! Rendezvous." Words can't express how meaningful it was for the team to meet and get to know each other in person. It was powerful! The first event of the rendezvous was dinner with special guest Tony Nadal (a company commander featured in the book, *We Were Soldiers Once...and Young).* After dinner, Tony took us to the Vietnam memorial where we gathered around him in the cold January night. He shined a light on panel #13, illuminating the names of his fallen warriors. When he was done telling their stories, he turned to us and said: "When I returned from Vietnam, no one asked me what I had learned. Your team is changing that legacy by asking the question and providing combat leaders a way to share what they learn. Keep it up!"

Building a team is a never-ending process as individual availability changes and as new members become active. In building your team, start small and intentionally connect with and grow a network of people who are passionate about your topic. Be always on the lookout for talent, and seize every opportunity you have to invite people onto the team. If a member posts a comment or submits content that reveals their expertise and passion, connect with them. Thank them for contributing and invite them to join the team! As a result, they will find meaning and have a new opportunity to live out their professional calling, and other members will benefit from what they bring to the table.

Organizing the Online Space

There are many ways to organize the online space of a professional forum, and our own organizing principles have changed over the years. In whatever way you decide to organize your forum space, it should be well thought out because it will influence the experience that your members have and

> **First Steps For Forum Leaders**
>
> ✓ Setting Direction
>
> ✓ Building A Team
>
> ➢ **Organizing the Online Space**

impact the way they think about effectiveness in their jobs. We currently use a topic-based organization, or taxonomy, meaning that CompanyCommand.army.mil is organized by topics.[9] In order to arrive at our current set of main topics, we asked ourselves, and hundreds of officers in different small-group settings, to answer this question:

---

[9] Taxonomy sounds "big and scary," but it really just boils down to the idea of dividing a Web site into topics or categories. Initially, CompanyCommand.com was "sectional based," meaning it was organized according to the type of information. For example, "Tools," "Ideas & Stories," and "Conversations." The main problem with this is that finding all the information about a specific topic is difficult. There might be excellent content about "Convoy Operations," for example, in each of the sections without any integration among them.

*What does a company-level unit need to be able to
do in order to be effective?*

Out of these conversations emerged a list of main topics: leadership, warfighting, training, fitness, force protection, maintenance, supply, and soldiers & families.

In addition to being able to find all types of knowledge (documents, conversations, etc.) in one place, this way of organizing has the potential to influence how officers think about the practice of company command. In the process of engaging in the professional forum and reading content and conversations across these critical topics, members learn—they become more effective. They also gain access to leaders who have vast experience in the different topics.

Topic leads similarly frame out their topic and identify its most important aspects. In doing this, a topic lead might ask questions such as:

- *What are the essential elements within my topic— elements that company commanders must "Be, Know, Do" in order to be effective?*

- *What are the top three issues right now for commanders in this topic?*

- *What experiences are commanders engaged in currently or preparing for that we can have an impact on?*

For example, in the *Leadership* topic, Mark Derber identified leader development as an essential aspect of leading a company effectively, and he broke it out as a sub-topic. This way of organizing focuses his efforts and drives content collection, conversation, and connections within the topic. For example, he is always on the lookout for counseling tools and leader-development ideas, and he and his team ask questions and otherwise create conversations dealing with things like initial counseling of lieutenants and the commander/first sergeant relationship. Additionally, he recruits experienced leaders to be contacts in this area.

Over time, the way a topic is organized—and those subjects that are deemed most important—will change or expand. Prior to the war in Iraq, CC had no content on convoy operations. Since the war began, however, topic lead Dean Dominique has led the charge to generate content on convoy ops. As a result, members can now access the *Convoy Operations Handbook* produced by a JRTC O/C and forum member; the *Convoy Leader Training Handbook* published by MPRI; the *Convoy Leader's Handbook* produced by CASCOM; a convoy operations TTP presentation prepared by a commander in Iraq; a convoy LPD put together by a company commander; a convoy operations' checklist tool contributed by a different commander; a link to the *Tactical Convoy Homepage*; and a discussion forum on convoy operations. Thus, topic leads adapt their organizing framework to the environment company commanders are in.

Let's now go back to our conversation with Deborah, our MP topic lead. We would ask her to think through and articulate those things that are critical to MP company commander effectiveness. By including her command contacts and pointmen in this conversation, she will develop a thorough organizing framework for the MP rally point. The framework will influence the type of content, conversation, and connections that emerge and, in the end, will impact the value that members gain through the forum.

*****

Action Summary—Chapter 7
First Steps: Direction, Team, Organizing Framework

	Process Questions	Principles and Practices
DIRECTION **Purpose** **Vision** **Values**	• Why do we exist? • Whom are we serving? • What future do we want to create? • How do we want to live on a day-to-day basis?	• There is power in having laser beam-like focus. • Say "no" to *good* in order to say "yes" to *great*. • *Who* is in the conversation changes the nature *of* the conversation. • We create our future.
TEAM **Initial Core Team**	• Who would we love to work with in this endeavor? • Who has already demonstrated by their actions a desire to share knowledge and to serve others?	• Two or three like-hearted leaders are more effective, more resilient, and better connected than one. • If *They* build it, *They* will come.
Pointman Concept	• Who are the members of the practice we are focused on serving—current as well as past and future? (and, Where are they located?) • Who do we already have relationships with? • Who do we need to develop relationships with?	• Reach the "many" through the "few." • Visualize where forum members are within the organization by using a NETMAP. • Leverage current relationships and continually develop new ones with a focus on adding value to the members of the professional forum.
Command Contacts	• Who has a lot of experience in our topic? • Who has expertise in a specific area that will provide value to members of our forum?	• Bring experienced leaders to bear for company commanders by making them available within an area of experience. • Be always on the lookout for leaders with specific expertise and recruit them to be contacts.

Making The Team A Team	• How effectively are we communicating with our team? • What can we do to improve our communication? • What can we do to increase team cohesion and camaraderie?	• Reinforce purpose, trust, and sense of impact through ongoing communication and building a sense of camaraderie within the team. • Building the team is a never- ending process. Continually recruit leaders to help out in specific high-impact areas of the forum.
ORGANIZING FRAMEWORK	• What does a leader in the practice or topic we are focused on need to be able to know and do in order to be effective? • What are the top three issues leaders are facing? • What experiences are commanders currently engaged in—or preparing for—that we can add value to?	• The way that the online space is organized will drive connections, conversation and content. • It will also impact on how leaders within the practice will think about effectiveness in their work.

Chapter 8

Making It Happen

Now that you have taken your first steps (setting direction, building a team, and creating an organizing framework), you are poised to do the ongoing work of a professional-forum leader; you are ready to "make it happen." In this chapter, we will climb into the trenches of the operation, getting a sense of the work a topic lead does day to day. We will also lay out a set of ideas that you can put in your rucksack—practical ideas you can select from as you seek to serve and add value to company commanders.

To accomplish this, let us go back to our MP topic lead, whom we introduced in the previous chapter. When we left off with that conversation, Deborah was launching the *MP Commander* rally point. It is now six months later and she is exchanging emails with an experienced topic lead, Rob Mitchell, who started the EOD rally point.

From: Rob
To: Deborah
Subject: Just check'n in

I was just checking out the *MP Commander* rally point and figured I'd send you an email. How are things going?

From: Deborah
To: Rob
Subject: Re: Just check'n in

Hey Rob, thanks for the note. It was REAL slow at first, but things are picking up. I got a cool note last night from someone who just took command in Iraq telling me that the stuff on the rally point really helped him out. Feedback like that makes it worthwhile, you know. I'm really busy with work lately, and sometimes I'm not sure if I'm using my time with the forum wisely.

From: Rob
To: Deborah
Subject: Just check'n in

Very nice on the note from the guy in combat. That kind of input is what keeps me fired up too. Say a little more about the time issue, so I can make sure I understand watcha mean.

From: Deborah
To: Rob
Subject: Re: Just check'n in

I'm totally onboard with what we are doing, but I'm always wondering if I'm doing enough. Between my job (recently took command of my second company), my family, and other commitments, I'm stretched thin. Sometimes, I feel frustrated or even guilty about the whole thing.

From: Rob
To: Deborah
Subject: Just check'n in

I've been there myself, Deb! Sometimes, I don't have time to do ANYTHING on the site for two weeks—it's a fact of life given work and family, etc. Every one of us TLs goes through cycles, and that is totally ok. That's one reason it's so important that we operate as a team. A "lot of littles make a lot." It's cool to think about the impact that our team can have over time if we each consistently do a little.

Here's one thought to chew on: At first, I felt success was if every EOD CO was actively participating ☺—now, I put my efforts into connecting with 8-12 members. A small and very committed group of active members can create amazing value. I'm always surprised to find out how someone I didn't even think knew about the forum was really benefiting from it.

From: Deborah
To: Rob
Subject: Re: Just check'n in

That's encouraging to hear. I like your point on going deep with a few relationships. What else has worked for you? No one has really told me what I should be doing...what is it that you actually do?

From: Rob
To: Deborah
Subject: Re: Just check'n in

LoL ☺—I'm dying laughing 'cause it took me months before I figured out what the heck I should be doing. Eventually, I developed a little battle rhythm. I'm attaching it here, with some notes for you—hope it helps.   ATTACHMENT: **TL Battle Rhythm**

There's more ;-) but hopefully this will give you some ideas. I think having a plan (one that fits in with your life) is key. Last but not least, we all learn by doing—just run with it and experiment. See what works best for you. AND HAVE FUN!

From: Deborah
To: Rob
Subject: Re: Just check'n in

TOO COOL Rob! ...wish I had your battle rhythm 6 months ago. In that document, I saw something about a Topic-Lead Rucksack. What is it, and how can I get a hold of it?

From: Rob
To: Deborah
Subject: Re: Just check'n in

The TL Rucksack is a collection of tried-and-true topic lead TTPs—kinda like our "battle drill" book. A couple of the ideas are ones I developed ☺. It ain't the be-all-to-end-all, but it's quick and jogs my thinking. I'm figuring you will see something in it that you will want to try. Oh, and I almost forgot, you can download the "rucksack" from the *On Fire! CC Team Blog*.

From: Deborah
To: Rob
Subject: Re: Just check'n in

I'm going to go check it out now! I'll let you know how it goes.

See next page

Topic Lead Battle Rhythm

Daily (or as possible)

> If any threads are new or need facilitation, I take a moment to respond in some way: maybe I'll email the person, or post a reply, or I also might email an experienced leader—like one of the EOD command contacts—asking him to join the conversation.

❑ Check the discussions within the EOD rally point.

❑ Check my CC "in box" to see if any members submitted content that needs to be approved.

> I will often review content and approve it to be loaded to the EOD commander space at that moment. I then write the content submitter a personal note, thanking them for their contribution.

Weekly

❑ Check out the *On Fire! CC Team Blog*.

> I read the team update, get new ideas, & participate in discussions there. Great place to ask questions, too.

❑ Check out other sections of CC.mil.

> I like to participate as I can outside of my topic, like in the main page discussions. Also, by looking around the site every week, I get to see what other TLs have going on and get good ideas that I bring into the EOD forum. I was checking out the MP rally point, which made me think of emailing you.

Monthly/Quarterly

❑ Develop a survey for EOD cdrs.

> I send a survey out via email to EOD rally point members quarterly and then post responses and facilitate a priority discussion about the subject of the survey. My goal is to have one priority discussion going at all times and this is a key way I do that.

❑ Select one activity from the *Topic-Lead* Rucksack and implement it.

> For example, last month I interviewed an experienced EOD commander and posted his interview along with a link to his dog tag on the EOD main page.

*****

We now leave our MP topic lead to present to you the contents of the "Topic-Lead Rucksack."

Topic-Lead Rucksack

This rucksack is intended to equip topic leads with ideas as they connect leaders, create conversations, and develop content.

The practices in this rucksack are tools of the *topic-lead trade*, all designed with the end state—improving company commander effectiveness—in mind.

Feature A Forum Member
Recruit A Member To Keep A Commander Log
Recruit A Command Contact
Communicate With A Forum Member
Send Out A Monthly Update/Newsletter
Feature Content
Conduct An Email Survey
Interview A Forum Member
Facilitate a Leader to Leader (L2L)
Develop a Quiz or a Command Challenge
Find and Link to Content From Other Sources
Facilitate A Priority Conversation
Create Context Around Content
Send A Welcome Letter To New Members

Feature A Forum Member

Featuring a forum member introduces the professional forum to itself and adds a sense of personal connection. It also creates awareness of who members are and what experiences they have to offer. This awareness facilitates connections that would otherwise not be possible.

You can identify members to feature by looking at those who have recently participated in the discussion forums or submitted content. You can also search member dog tags, looking for specific types of experiences that would be valuable to have featured. Rotating featured members every two to four weeks is about right. Work with the member you will feature to add additional information to their dog tag—such as an updated photo, recent experiences, and even a mini interview you conduct with them. Finally, follow up by mailing a team hat or other piece of CC team gear to thank them.

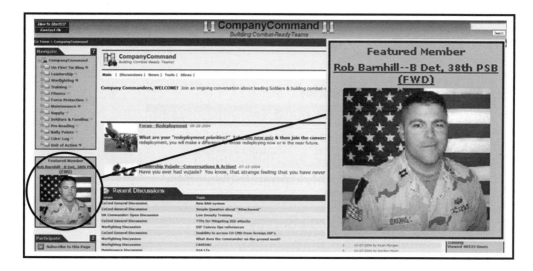

Note from a commander who was featured on CC:

"Thanks for highlighting me on CC. It was a thrill getting emails from friends and fellow officers. I also got to answer many questions from leaders who are preparing to deploy here to Iraq. Thanks again!" –Sebastian Pastor

Featuring a member can also draw attention to different areas of the forum. For example, Rob Barnhill is a command contact for the *Soldiers & Family* topic—so, when he was featured on CC, we highlighted this on his dog tag and hyperlinked members directly to that topic.

*Topic-Lead Tip: Nominate a member to feature on the main page. Also, feature members in your topic. Even without a picture, you can highlight the name (linked to the dog tag) at the top of your topic or even in a threaded discussion.

Recruit A Member To Keep a Commander Log

The *Commanders' Log* is a section of CC.mil where company commanders are capturing what they are learning in real time. Participating commanders have their own space that serves as their individual commander log. When they post an entry to their log, the entry is also visible in the collective commanders' log.

While commander logs make the experience of current company commanders available to others, the commander keeping the log may get the most out of the experience. Recruit forum members who are currently in or are preparing for company command. In the process, share with them how the log will provide value to them as well as to the rest of the profession.

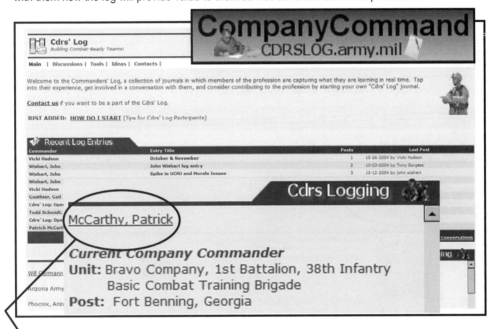

"I will journal my command experience here in the *Cdrs' Log* to capture my experience commanding B/1-38 Infantry, which is a basic training unit at Fort Benning, Georgia. I have been a long-time member of CompanyCommand.com and believe in the responsibility we all have as professionals to contribute what we are learning and experiencing to our comrades. My desire in doing this is to capture my experience as well as to get feedback from other commanders. So, if you are reading this, please know that I would count it a privilege if you posted a comment, question, or idea for me. Thanks!" –**Pat McCarthy**

BONUS: Topic leads can designate individual commander logs so that posts are included in the most recent discussion comments for that topic. For example, Todd Schmidt's log entries appear in both the *Afghan Commander* topic as well as the *ADA* rally point since he is an ADA commander currently deployed to Afghanistan.

Recruit A Command Contact

Command contacts are forum members who have a depth of experience in a particular topic and who make themselves available to company commanders. They respond to questions, identify knowledge gaps for their topic, and do much of the work of connecting members. Command contacts, along with their respective topic leads, are thought leaders for their topic.

Each topic will ideally have a team of contacts featured. In this example, Maria Chamorro, Rob Barnhill, Sean Fisher, and Ray Kimball serve as a command contacts for the *Soldiers & Families* topic. These four committed professionals have a vision for providing the best resources available for company commanders on issues related to taking care of Soldiers and families.

Communicate With A Forum Member

Communicating one-on-one with members is a topic lead's bread and butter. When a member posts a comment or submits content in your topic, connect with them. Thank them for contributing and get to know them. Find out how you can serve them and how they might want to contribute. Members totally appreciate this! The number one reason active members cite for becoming more involved is a personal connection with a CC team member—even if it is a simple note of appreciation for their participation.

See the example below of an email communication between CC topic lead Ray Kimball and a forum member (Bradd) who submitted a quality comment to a grief-counseling discussion thread:

> Bradd,
> I'm the *Soldiers & Families* topic lead for CompanyCommand. I just read your posting on Chris Engen's grief counseling resource thread. Wow! The notifications and funerals must have been brutal, especially being geographically separated as you were from the platoons. I admire your willingness to talk about it, especially as you're transitioning to the new force structure. (The recce troops look like they're going to be exciting places to be!) Could I prevail upon you to list yourself as a contact for our *Casualty Operations* topic? I have lots of technical info there, but no one who's gone through what you have and can provide professional experience and wisdom to others. Just let me know. As always, if there's anything I or the rest of the team can do for you, just let me know.
> —Ray Kimball for the CompanyCommand Team

Commo Tips for Professional-Forum Leaders (From Chapter Seven)

✓ Continually share purpose. Reinforce why the professional forum exists and whom the team is serving.

✓ Specifically communicate the impact that the person is having, and thank them for it. Without feedback, people may be unaware of the value they are providing, the difference they are making.

✓ Pass on a tip or lesson learned.

✓ If the person doesn't have something specific "to do" for the team, get them engaged. Describe what that person can do—something that will make a real and practical difference—and ask them to do it.

✓ Convey a genuine interest in the person as a person, beyond just their work with the forum.

Send Out A Monthly Update/Newsletter

A newsletter/update establishes a connection with forum members, and it provides a "push" of available knowledge. Extremely busy members who might not otherwise go to the forum will get energized by an effective newsletter. There is no recipe on how to do this, but we try to include a couple of common elements:

- ✓ A thought piece that encourages and challenges leaders in their practice of leadership.
- ✓ Areas that the CC team is focused on and looking for input on.
- ✓ Highlight exciting new content and team developments.
- ✓ Highlight forum members who have made an exceptional contribution since the last newsletter.

Excerpt from the CC Oct/Nov 2003 Newsletter:

NOV FOCUS: Our focus on CompanyCommand.com during November continues to build around the subject of "Training." We need you to **go to that section** of the site and to contribute your ideas and experiences in that area.

CMD QUIZ: The *Cmd Quiz* for October was, "How does training fit into the operational environment?" The discussion around the question was awesome, and we encourage you to **check out a summary of that discussion.** Stay tuned for the next quiz that will be up on the site this week.

CMD CHALLENGE: Rob McCormick—who commanded an Avenger Battery in Iraq—has developed a new *Command Challenge* for you. It revolves around this scenario: "You have just been alerted and will deploy your unit to Iraq. You have four months to get ready and—oh by the way—the tasks you will be performing and the equipment you will be using are brand new to your unit." **Take the challenge**. Then, share your thinking by posting a discussion comment.

MEMBER RECOGNITION: During the month of October, many new people stepped up to the plate to actively contribute to the profession via CC. We would like to recognize some of them here: Bradford Cary, Angela Crist, Rob McCormick, Rob Griggs, Raymond Kimball, Jay Miseli, and Brett Patron. Thank you very much!

This is your professional forum. If you would like to participate in a more active way, please let us know. **[email us]**

CONTENT YOU DON'T WANNA MISS:

CompanyCommand.com is not a repository for "stuff"—It is an ongoing professional conversation specifically focused around Company Command. Whether you submit an article or tool, post a discussion comment, or have a conversation with a bud as a result of something you read, you are participating in an ongoing conversation. When you read and use content, take the time to post a comment to that content. Add value to it, thank the person who contributed it, and ask questions about it. With that in mind, here are just a few of the incredible things we recommend you check out:

o **Josh Wright, "Training Food for Thought As You Prepare for Combat"** Josh commanded A/3-15 IN in OIF and is now in command of E/9 CAV (BRT)

o **Robert McCormick, "Training Scenarios/Tips for deployment to Iraq in support of OIF"** Rob, an Avenger Battery Commander in OIF shares ideas on training scenarios for units preparing to deploy. Also, see the **"Training TTPs: What is Working Discussion"**

o **Pete Kilner, "Ongoing Interviews with Battle-Tested C-L Leaders"**

o **"Video Interviews with Battle-Tested C-L Leaders"** **Clay Lyle, Mark Brzozowski, Dan Van Kirk, and SFC Ford.** This is an amazing OPD package that includes video interview footage taken by Pete Kilner while on the ground in Iraq.

Note: The CC newsletters go out via email to all members and are also archived and available via CC.mil

---

*Topic-Lead Tip: Create a running email distribution list of every member who participates in your topic. Send them a monthly or bi-monthly update for your topic that highlights new content and gives them a direct connection to what is going on. Let them know when a member posts an important question, and keep them in the loop. Create a sense of community around your topic, and invite participation. You will be amazed how this one practice will unleash members on your topic and create amazing value for company commanders. (And, it is fun!)

Feature Content

Featuring new or particularly relevant content ensures member awareness of key knowledge in the forum. This practice makes it easier for busy company commanders to find new and important content, and it shapes the experience that members have.

Below is a screen shot from the *EOD Commander* rally point on CC.mil. Rob Mitchell, *EOD* topic lead, has featured content both within his section of the site and content from other sections of the site that he believes EOD commanders would benefit from.

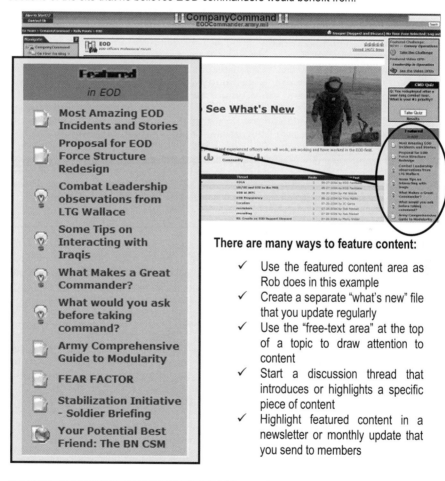

There are many ways to feature content:

✓ Use the featured content area as Rob does in this example
✓ Create a separate "what's new" file that you update regularly
✓ Use the "free-text area" at the top of a topic to draw attention to content
✓ Start a discussion thread that introduces or highlights a specific piece of content
✓ Highlight featured content in a newsletter or monthly update that you send to members

Thinking of yourself as a magazine editor and company commanders as subscribers can be helpful when it comes to thinking about featuring content. Presentation of content is inextricably linked to how it will be received by members, so think through how you can best use space, color, and graphics to grab readers' attention and deliver value to them.

Conduct An Email Survey

People respond when asked a question. Their likelihood of responding increases when they know (and trust) the person asking, when they are asked directly, and when they believe that their input is valued and will be put to use.

This is an example of a question that CC topic lead Jay Miseli crafted and then emailed to a group of officers who had re-deployed their companies from combat operations:

Imagine you have the opportunity to sit down with 8-12 company commanders who just returned from an OIF deployment. They've been gone for a year, and they just completed the redeployment process. Many of them have not had a chance to think much beyond getting their Soldiers and equipment safely home. One of them asks you this question: **"If you were a company commander in my shoes just finishing a major redeployment, what would be your top priority? And, why?"**
Note: Your response will be most valuable if you can include a story or elaborate a little with some details to provide context and to make your input as meaningful as possible. As I mentioned before, we will post your input via the CC forum; also, some members of our team are leading a workshop with Company-Level Leaders in Germany 27-29 September (one workshop a day). Most of the attendees will have JUST RETURNED from OIF. If we get your input in time, we will include it in the workshops, which would be really awesome. On behalf of all the leaders who will benefit from your experience, thank you for responding! ...and thanks for your time.
                                                                                      –Jay Miseli for the CC Team

---

Leaders strongly desire to share what they know! Within days, twenty experienced commanders responded to Jay's question. Jay fed the responses into an ongoing discussion on CC.mil about redeployment priorities, and the CC team packaged them into an article used at a workshop with C-L leaders in Germany. The following is one of many responses received:

Jay,
It is important to decompress your Soldiers under a controlled environment. I highly discourage any plan to cut Soldiers loose on block leave immediately upon redeployment. Also, do not rest on your laurels upon redeployment from combat—you may return to combat sooner than you expect. So make a plan to be ready. In an ideal world, I recommend something like this: **Week 1-2:** Reverse SRP and Re-integration Training. Re-establishment of barracks and S&A facilities. CDR/ 1SG: Develop a reset training plan ICW the Squadron reset plan. **Week 3-4:** Block Leave. **Week 5-6:** Receive Equipment, equipment maintenance. Establish accountability of equipment, update H/R's. Re-establish vigor in PT program. **Week 6-7:** Individual training such as weapons qualification. Begin to "reset" the Soldiers and Unit and get ready for the next deployment. —Mike Kirkpatrick (I/3/2 ACR and HHT/1/2 ACR, Fort Polk & OIF)

---

*Topic-Lead Tip: Craft a question every other month and send it out to everyone you know with relevant experience. Then, package the responses as content in your topic.

Interview A Forum Member

Interviews are one of the most effective ways we've found to create quality content and build relationships with experienced leaders. The sky is the limit in terms of the medium used for the interview—we primarily use web-based surveys, email, phone, and face-to-face interaction (to include the use of video).

Trent Upton
Cdr, A/2-5 CAV, Iraq
Interviewed one week after taking command in Iraq

1. What was your toughest leadership challenge, and how did you address it? Improving information flow and motivation in my company. The two are tied closely together. Soldiers always execute more effectively when they know why they are doing something. I have emphasized communication within the company so we can "see ourselves". I implemented [...] far: Nightly meetings and talking to my soldiers several times a day. During the nightly meetings [...] AARs of the last 24hrs' missions, cover operations for the next 24 and 48hrs, identify resources [...] outstanding issues and suspenses, and issue guidance and priorities of work...

This interview excerpt consists of six questions we ask in our combat-leader interviews. While we may ask more questions, these questions form the foundation. This interview is web-based and can be accessed from CC.mil. Team members are able to email the interview link to leaders, asking them to contribute their hard-earned knowledge in this way.

2. Will your experiences in OIF change the way you lead and train soldiers? Yes. I ha[...] been in command for a week at this time. During this short time, I have led my company on two [...] search mission, in addition to executing daily CMO patrols in sector. Focus on the basics. Ba[...] medical training, etc. We conduct a high amount of decentralized, platoon level operations. Train[...]

3. What do you think best prepared you for the challenge of leadership in combat? O[...] company commanders as well as my Battalion and Brigade Commander. Be a "sponge". Listen [...] AO. I spent my first three months in Iraq on staff. During that time I always paid close attentio[...] that worked and those that did not, and how commanders dealt with the ever-changing environme[...]

4. What advice do you have for leaders preparing for OIF? Focus on the basics. Battle d[...] and advanced marksmanship, combat-lifesaver training, and PT.

5. What image, event, or feeling do you think you will remember most in 50 years? [...] advertised. The will execute to their fullest capacity under harsh conditions and in an ever-chang[...] joking around in the barracks, having as much fun as possible in the FOB; the next they will be r[...] focused on their mission. After completing their mission, they return to the FOB, finish refit requir[...] boys" again in the barracks. Their flexibility and resiliency is amazing and inspiring to me.

6. Do you have any additional thoughts you'd like to share with the profession? Company Command, all seven days so far, is by far the best opportunity I have had in the Army. Taking command in combat has got to be the most challenging way to start. If you end up taking command while in theater, don't wait to make changes you think are necessary. If I had assumed command in garrison, my own style would have leaned toward taking a week or two to get a feel for what is or is not working in the company and then decide what needed to be changed. I don't, and you won't, have that luxury in a combat environment. You have to come in, have a long talk with your 1SG, XO, Platoon Leaders, and Platoon Sergeants, talk to as many of your soldiers as possible, use your eyes and ears, and make a quick assessment...   [read the complete interview via the *Warfighting* topic on CC.mil]

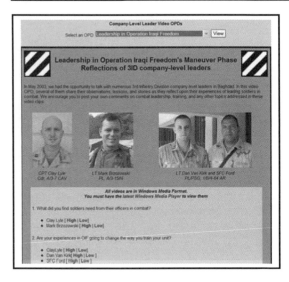

In order to create timely and relevant resources, members of the CC team have physically traveled to meet with and learn from company-level leaders on the ground in combat. This video interview is one example. Two keys to a successful interview include preparing the questions before-hand with the interviewee and keeping responses to each question short and focused (1-2 minutes).

We package some video interviews as OPDs with other content such as maps and links to related articles.

Facilitate a Leader 2 Leader (L2L)

A Leader 2 Leader (L2L) is a gathering of Company-Level leaders who come together to share their knowledge and experience and to talk about things that matter when it comes to leading Soldiers and building combat-ready units. Some examples include:

✓ Facilitating a local gathering of company commanders committed to supporting and learning from each other.
✓ Participating in a Division's Pre-Command/1SG Course. For example, the CC team has delivered a company-level leadership workshop at the 10th Mountain Course for the past couple of years.
✓ Traveling to conferences to facilitate workshops such as what the team did at the Land Combat Expo with Dan Hubbard (See Chapter Two).

Imagine small groups of company commanders across the Army meeting routinely at their units to share what they are learning and to spur each other on. You can see how the impact gets punched up a notch when leaders capture what they are learning at their local gatherings and share with the profession via CC.mil. If you are meeting with leaders in your neck of the woods, let us know and we will do whatever we can to help support your efforts.

The *Pro-Reading* program serves as a catalyst for conversation at local L2L gatherings. Imagine organizing a gathering of leaders at your post/unit to talk about a book and then making what you are learning available to the rest of the Army through CC.mil.

Let us know and we'll order your books!

 **Take the Pro-Reading Challenge!** *Mike Runey 06-03-2004*

Want to move your OPD program into full throttle in the midst of high-optempo environments? Check this out.

Pro Reading has a direct impact on your unit effectiveness. **[Why *is* ProReading important?]**

We want to create a space for you to gather with your leaders in a conversation about leadership, warfighting, and those things that directly impact on your unit's effectiveness. If this sounds good to you, take the **ProReading Challenge** -- you and your leaders will be glad you did.

---

*Topic-Lead Tip: Invite two or three CC members to meet over lunch once every month or two to talk about company command and how to advance the profession via CC.mil. If you organize a L2L in a different location (e.g., your last post), we will resource your trip. Let us know how we can unleash you in service of company commanders!

Develop A Quiz Or A Command Challenge

Both the *Command Quiz* and the *Command Challenge* sections of the site are designed to be catalysts for conversations (on and off-line). Typically, a member will nominate a new quiz or challenge; it is then shared across the CC team, where it is further refined and shaped until it is posted on CC.mil. In the process of kicking it around the team, a lot of great ideas are shared that the pointman on the quiz or challenge often incorporates or feeds into the online discussion once it is posted.

Command Challenge:

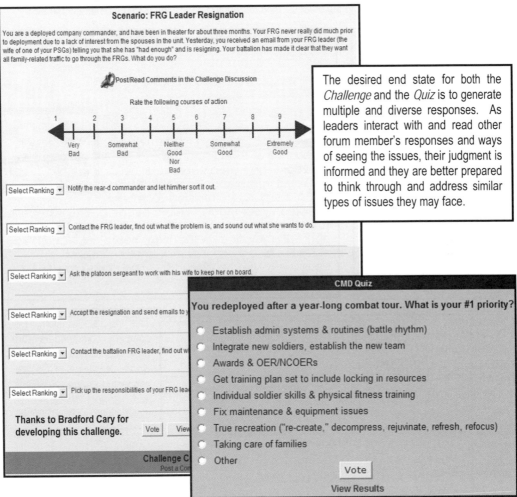

Scenario: FRG Leader Resignation

You are a deployed company commander, and have been in theater for about three months. Your FRG never really did much prior to deployment due to a lack of interest from the spouses in the unit. Yesterday, you received an email from your FRG leader (the wife of one of your PSGs) telling you that she has "had enough" and is resigning. Your battalion has made it clear that they want all family-related traffic to go through the FRGs. What do you do?

Post/Read Comments in the Challenge Discussion

Rate the following courses of action

1   2   3   4   5   6   7   8   9

Very Bad — Somewhat Bad — Neither Good Nor Bad — Somewhat Good — Extremely Good

[Select Ranking ▼] Notify the rear-d commander and let him/her sort it out.

[Select Ranking ▼] Contact the FRG leader, find out what the problem is, and sound out what she wants to do.

[Select Ranking ▼] Ask the platoon sergeant to work with his wife to keep her on board.

[Select Ranking ▼] Accept the resignation and send emails to y

[Select Ranking ▼] Contact the battalion FRG leader, find out w

[Select Ranking ▼] Pick up the responsibilities of your FRG lea

Thanks to Bradford Cary for developing this challenge. [Vote] [View

Challenge C
Post a Com

The desired end state for both the *Challenge* and the *Quiz* is to generate multiple and diverse responses. As leaders interact with and read other forum member's responses and ways of seeing the issues, their judgment is informed and they are better prepared to think through and address similar types of issues they may face.

CMD Quiz

You redeployed after a year-long combat tour. What is your #1 priority?

○ Establish admin systems & routines (battle rhythm)
○ Integrate new soldiers, establish the new team
○ Awards & OER/NCOERs
○ Get training plan set to include locking in resources
○ Individual soldier skills & physical fitness training
○ Fix maintenance & equipment issues
○ True recreation ("re-create," decompress, rejuvinate, refresh, refocus)
○ Taking care of families
○ Other

[Vote]

View Results

*Topic-Lead Tip: Develop a challenge or quiz based on your own experience that is tied to your topic. Doing so infuses energy and advances the state of your topic.

Find and Link to Content From Other Sources

Imagine if company commanders were connected through CC.mil to everything that could help them be more effective commanders? CC members make this happen by constantly scanning for quality content that will deliver value to current company commanders and then linking to it via CC.mil. Examples of excellent sources include the *Center for Army Lessons Learned* (CALL) and the branch journals. This becomes especially important for busy commanders who might not necessarily read every journal. For example, a Field Artillery commander may not be aware that an exceptional article on company-level training management just came out in *Armor Magazine*. Creating awareness about this article on CC.mil connects many leaders to quality content that they would not otherwise know about. And, in the process, members of the profession become better connected.

This example is from the *Afghan Cdr* topic on CC.mil. Jim Isenhower identified a need—up-to-date OEF TTPs—and then searched to find quality resources that would speak to that need. Many COs simply would not know this great resource existed without its being featured on CC.mil.

Come across a great article that is relevant to company commanders? Let's link to it via CC.mil!

CALL on OPN Enduring Freedom!

Jim Isenhower 05-17-2003

Use the Army's CALL for Enduring Freedom Lessons!

Use this link to visit the CALL access page: https://call2.leavenworth.army.mil/. Select "Operation Enduring Freedom" and then enter your personal information to gain access to CALL's site. Permission to enter is based on your input, verified by the DEERs database. It's very easy and CALL offers some great lessons and TTP, including methods for operating at high altitudes and a great Natick brief on soldier equipment and asociated lessons during the 101st's fight in Afghanistan.

 ### Chasing the Mythical Commander's Week, by CPT Chris Connolly (Armor Magazine)

One cdr's ideas on how to make the most of limited training ti[me] the Nov/Dec 2001 Armor Magazine issue.

Website Type   Visit the Armor Magazine homepage at: http://www.knox.army.mil/center/ocoa/ArmorMag/index.htm

Website (URL)   http://www.knox.army.mil/center/ocoa/ArmorMag/nd01/6cdrsweek01.pdf

↩ Post Comment on this page.

This is a "win-win" for company commanders and professional sources like *Armor Magazine*. COs are connected to quality content and *Armor Magazine* is more widely read.

*Topic-Lead Tip: Instead of linking to a large document that members will have to search through to find the nugget you intended them to see, it is sometimes more effective to excerpt the key point while including a link to the complete article/document so members can read it if they want to.

Facilitate A Priority Conversation

Topic leads identify important issues, frame them in the form of questions, and then take action to generate conversations that truly impact company commander effectiveness—they create and facilitate "priority conversations."

Imagine the impact on the profession if one priority conversation was happening on every CC.mil topic. With this in mind, our goal is for topic leads to always have one priority conversation in progress and one that they are preparing to launch (see Chapter Nine).

Great questions energize professional forums and move members to action!

Priority conversations generate knowledge, increase company commander effectiveness, and advance the profession.

Priority Conversation Primer

1st, craft a question (get your team involved)
- ✓ What question, if asked in my topic, could generate conversation and deliver significant value to current COs?
- ✓ What is an emerging issue for COs that—if they were talking about it—would prepare them and make them more effective?
- ✓ What question would be worth investing my energy in generating conversation about for two months?

2nd, launch and facilitate the conversation
- ✓ Get the word out about the new question
- ✓ Personally invite members to participate
- ✓ Facilitate the tone of the conversation
- ✓ Create interaction between members, building on key insights and comments
- ✓ Broaden or re-focus the conversation
- ✓ Summarize the conversation

Example: Kevin Butler, *Training* topic lead, crafted the following question to generate conversation about the important topic of convoy operations:

Convoy operations are receiving more attention as of late. I would be interested in hearing your comprehensive/innovative ideas to train convoy operations, particularly those in CS/CSS units.

Instead of leaving participation to chance, the CC team took action to launch the conversation: A search of CC member dog tags, looking for leaders who had specific experience in convoy operations, quickly led the team to over thirty leaders who listed convoy operations experience in OIF/OEF on their dog tags! Personally inviting these members to participate in this conversation—to share their experience—ensured this priority conversation got off to an exceptional start.

Create Context Around Content

Content becomes especially valuable when it is surrounded by rich context that gives it meaning and brings it to life. A *PowerPoint* slide with a lesson learned, stripped of all the contextual knowledge underpinning the lesson, is relatively meaningless. However, add knowledge about the person (via linking their dog tag to the content) and include background information about the situation in which the lesson was learned—the outcome, the time-frame, and who was involved—and the content is sure to make a greater impact.

What does context do?

- ✓ It gives people a better sense for what they will get if they click on the file.
- ✓ It personalizes the content so that it isn't just static information—it conveys personality and voice in a way that is missing with a stand-alone document. It draws people in.
- ✓ It helps communicate the underlying principles involved in the application of the knowledge, allowing members to better apply it to their unique situations.
- ✓ It situates the content and communicates greater meaning.

To create context around content, topic leads often interview the member, asking questions like:	Other ways that topic leads create context around existing content:
✓ Is there a story behind how this idea/tool was developed? ✓ How has it made a difference for you and/or your unit? Any examples? ✓ Do you have any advice for new COs about how to best implement this idea/tool?	✓ Ask the member to add the context himself ✓ Post a discussion comment to the actual content and spark a conversation about it ✓ Add pictures, graphics, and color ✓ Link the content together with other related content (or other content from the same person)

Imagine finding a piece of content in the *Supply* topic titled "Fuel-Tracking Chart." You may or may not open the attached excel spreadsheet. Now imagine seeing the same content with the following context provided with it:

"I developed this fuel tracking chart after I had some problems forecasting fuel on my first major FTX—a rotation in the box at the NTC. In fact, one of the armor units I was supposed to resupply ended up being stuck in their assembly area for the final attack because they never got their needed fuel. Ouch! I took input from my platoon leaders and NCOs and came up with the attached tool. I just returned from Iraq and let me tell you, it worked and kept me straight on fuel. Considering that my company is responsible for fueling the entire Brigade TF, it was important that we got it right."

Topic leads take the initiative to create this kind of context around content. It takes time, but IT IS WORTH THE EFFORT!

Examples of Context Around Content

Context: That which surrounds something and gives it greater meaning.

Example #1: Topic lead creates context for an existing tool:

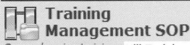

Training Management SOP

Comprehensive training management SOP for a Company-Level Unit.

Hill-Training SOP.doc
DOWNLOAD NOW

A MUST READ! This is the most comprehensive SOP for company-level training management and execution that we have seen. One example in the SOP is the training plan shell for platoon leaders to submit to the CO--it is **EXCELLENT**.

Donn commanded an Air Assault Infantry Company in Korea and a Ranger Company in 1st Ranger Battalion. He submitted this product soon after CompanyCommand.com started, and it is probably the most used resource we have ever had on the site. **The profession thanks you Donn!**

Interesting SIDE BAR: We know one CPT who, when his 25th ID(L) barracks were completely redesigned, built his Company "War Room" to match the exact specifications that Donn Hill lays out in this Training SOP.

Then, David Polizzotti posts a comment to it, adding additional context:

"This is an absolutely outstanding tool for new commanders who find themselves walking into a unit with no training- management program. The SOP breaks everything down to the fundamentals and gives great examples of what certain products should look like. I modified it a little bit to make it Armor- company friendly, and it has worked magnificently! So well that I took it, changed it a bit more and have implemented it within my HHC. This is a solid product I would recommend to anyone."

Example #2: A member provides context up front, before he shares his excellent "advice":

One Tanker's Advice to Commanders Faced with Change
One leader's story of how his unit adapted for the OIF deployment

★★★★★
Viewed 243 times

Author	Aaron Munz	Branch	Armor
Organization	2-12 CAV	Date Added:	04-19-2004
Post	Ft Hood/Iraq		

One Tanker's Advice to Commanders Faced with Change

I am a tank company commander in 2-12 Cavalry, 2nd BCT, 1st Cavalry Division, currently deployed in Baghdad, Iraq. However I deployed without any tanks and we are currently equipped with M1114 Up-Armored HMMWVs. We call ourselves light cavalrymen. (I have drawn 4 M1A1 MBTs since arriving in Iraq to counter an increased IED Threat). The following is the training plan that my company developed and executed to transition from a high-intensity-conflict focused force into a lighter unit able to counter the terrorist threat and maneuver in the complex urban terrain of western Baghdad.

*Topic-Lead Tip: When a member submits content, ask yourself: "How could we make this content come to life? What additional context could take this content from **good to GREAT?**"

Send A Welcome Letter To New Members

A welcome letter is an opportunity to connect with new members: to communicate purpose, vision, values; to introduce them to the organizing framework of the online space; and to invite them to participate. A warm and purpose-driven welcome sets the tone for the new members' experience and influences their future participation.

The example below is an excerpt from the CC.mil welcome letter for new members.
*Underlined text is hyperlinked to the specific Web pages.

Welcome to the CompanyCommand Team. We want to give you some valuable background information and some insight into how you can plug into and get the most out of your CC forum.

As a current company commander (or an officer preparing for command or a past company commander who is committed to giving back to current commanders), we are pumped to have you on the team. This is your professional forum—it is much more than a Web site. By joining, you are gaining access to an amazing community of professionals who love Soldiers and are committed to building combat-ready teams. **Please participate, contribute, and tap into the experience of others.**

Note: You should have already received a password via email, and you have probably already logged on. Once you get logged in, you can change the password via the *"my preferences"* link on the lower-left menu. While there, you can select to receive emails from the CC Team in html format and also select the correct time zone.

The CompanyCommand space is organized around the "big rocks" of command that we call "Topics"—**Leadership, Warfighting, Training, Fitness, Supply, Maintenance, Force Protection, Soldiers & Family**. We also have an area specifically for **Professional Reading** and **FRG Leaders**, as well as the **Cdrs' Log**—where commanders are journaling their command experience. Some of your comrades are pulling together resources into a new topic called **Unit of Action** located via the main page. If you have any content that could help there, please join in.

If you are preparing for command, we recommend you check out the **"1st 90 Days"**, located under the **"Leadership"** topic.

Also, take a look at the **"Rally Point"** section where you will find forums for specific types of COs to connect and share ideas and lessons learned: e.g., ADA Commander, Engineer, EOD, Field Artillery, Headquarters, IET, Logistics, Medical, Military Intelligence, Military Police, OBC, Rear D, SBCT, SF, Signal, USAR, etc... **Please find *your* rally point and introduce yourself there.** *Note:* If you don't see a rally point for your type of command or branch, why not start one up! Let us know if you are interested.

Again, welcome to the team.

---

*Topic-Lead Tip: Develop a welcome note of your own that you send out to any member who posts a discussion comment or submits content to your topic for the first time. Doing so creates a connection, reinforces their participation, and shows them that their contributions are appreciated.

Chapter 9

Making the Most of Online Conversations

We pick up the conversation between Deborah, our MP rally point topic lead, and Rob Mitchell, our experienced topic lead. It is now several months after Rob introduced her to the *Topic-Lead Rucksack*.

From: Deborah
To: Rob
Subject: Worthwhile Conversations

Rob, long time no talk. Things have been rockin' on the MP forum. Along with the "topic-lead rucksack," I think the most beneficial TTP you gave me was to focus on growing a small but totally committed group of MP Commanders. Your tip helped shift my focus from trying to "do it all" to getting a few people totally engaged in the forum. They say that every great movement begins when 2-3 people who believe in something connect and start talking. Now I understand! The one thing I'm still wondering about though is the quality of online conversations. We have a good amount of discussion posts and people asking questions, but I just get the feeling that we are missing something.

From: Rob
To: Deborah
Subject: Re: Worthwhile Conversations

Way to go on growing a team of committed members. MP COs who experience the forum will be drawn to the sense of camaraderie and the level of knowledge that is being shared. Very cool! You mentioned "missing something" as far as the discussions. Whatcha mean by that?

From: Deborah
To: Rob
Subject: Re: Worthwhile Conversations

I guess I meant a couple of things really. First, I'm not sure I know what I'm doing when it comes to facilitating conversations—you know, getting people engaged in a way that adds real value. My guess is that we (MP COs) could be getting a LOT more outta the conversation side of things...and yet, I wonder if online conversations can ever come close to face-to-face ones.

From: Rob
To: Deborah
Subject: Re: Worthwhile Conversations

Wow! You are learning faster than I did, that's for sure. I think you are ready for the master topic lead course on facilitating online conversation. :-) OK, there isn't a course, but we did put together a sorta handbook for online facilitation. The way I see it, we are just scratching the surface on what is possible when it comes to productive conversations—the kind of conversations that directly impact on our learning and effectiveness. I'm psyched to know that other topic leads like you are seeing it too. Give me a day or two to scare up my handbook and I'll get you a copy...

What Makes For A Dynamic Conversation?

Imagine for a moment one of the best face-to-face conversations you've participated in. That conversation probably had a lot of energy and depth because people were engaged; they weren't simply repeating tired platitudes, but were thinking hard about issues that really mattered to them and generating new insights as the conversation progressed.

In that best face-to-face conversation, people seemed to build on each other's ideas so that what each person said was influenced by what the person before had said. It was not simple turn taking with each person stating their view, but rather each person was reshaping and altering what they would say next based on what others had said. The next speaker, in fact, often acknowledged or incorporated ideas of the previous speaker. As a person was speaking, she was watching the reactions of others to see if others were nodding in understanding, if they were agreeing, or if everyone was looking confused like they had no idea what the speaker was talking about.

A leader with good facilitation skills can play a vital role in fostering such a productive conversation. A skilled facilitator is totally present with the group, following the flow of the conversation while keeping an eye on the group's dynamics. When someone asks a question that seems to confuse others, the facilitator steps in to ask for clarification, then steers the discussion to someone who may know the answer.

In addition, the facilitator steps back from the conversation to ask big-picture questions: What are we not taking into consideration here? What are we avoiding? Have we come to agreement before we've explored all the possibilities? A facilitator works to make the conversation as productive as possible.

The same kind of dynamics that happen in the most productive face-to-face conversation also need to happen in an online conversation. And the task of the facilitator becomes even more important because online members can't pick up on the many cues they make use of when face-to-face—for example, checking around the room to see if everyone is engaged. In an online conversation, the facilitator becomes the eyes and ears of the group, helping everyone "see" what is happening in the conversation.

Questions Generate Action

Questions are catalysts for conversation in both face-to-face and online conversations. In fact, most of the conversations on CC.mil are generated by the questions that members ask. The professional forum thus counts on the community of members to participate—both by asking questions when they have them and by responding to questions when they have relevant knowledge and experience to share.

Although more and more members are indeed taking the initiative to participate, our experience has been that topic leads and command contacts play a crucial role in energizing the forum to respond to questions and in facilitating productive online conversations—the kind of conversations that create learning and increase member effectiveness. It is with this in mind that we created the *Online Facilitation Handbook* as a companion to the *Topic-Lead Rucksack.*

This companion to the *Topic-Lead Rucksack* is intended to equip topic leads and to help them make the most of online conversations.

The practices that follow are tools of the *topic lead trade*, all designed with the end state—improving company commander effectiveness—in mind.

Connecting leaders in conversation

Online Facilitation Handbook

Initial Assessment

Initial Response

Close the Loop

Priority Conversations

✓ **Launch the conversation**

✓ **Facilitate the tone of the conversation**

✓ **Create interaction between participants**

    1. Invite a member to build on his comment

    2. Invite other members to build upon a comment

    3. Uncover the reasoning behind comments

✓ **Broaden or re-focus the conversation**

    1. Invite a diversity of opinions

    2. Refocus lagging conversations

    3. Return to issues that have been bypassed

    4. Keep the conversation on track

    5. Energize the conversation

✓ **Summarize the conversation**

Initial Assessment

Is the question aligned with what CC is about, is it clearly stated with enough detail, and is it urgent?

Members, especially topic leads and command contacts, conduct an initial assessment when they read a new question or comment posted in the online discussion area. For one, they filter the question through the CC values.[1] For example, "Is the question positive and solutions-oriented?" "Is it laser-beam focused on company command, and will it

Aligned with what CC is about?

create a productive conversation that adds value to company commanders?" And, if not, "Could it be rephrased in a way that would lead to a productive conversation?" During this initial assessment, reading the person's dog tag can provide helpful context as far as who the person is and what content they have contributed in the past.

A second part of the initial assessment is whether or not the question is effectively communicated. A good question is clearly stated and includes enough detail to create the context required to answer it effectively. This may seem obvious; however, when a question is confusing or too general, members tend to ignore it. Take, for example, the question "Does anyone have information on

Clearly stated, with enough detail?

developing different leadership strategies?" It is unclear what the person is looking for. Without clarification, questions like this go unanswered and, if members do respond, their answers usually won't address the member's actual need.

A third aspect of the initial assessment has to do with how immediate the person's need is. We categorize questions that are significant as far as the impact an immediate response will provide as URGENT. For example, "One of my Soldiers was killed last night and I need an example letter of condolence." Members

URGENT?

recognize these questions for what they are and pull out all the stops to quickly respond.

---

[1] See CC values in Chapter 7, "First Steps for Professional-Forum Leaders."

Initial Response

*The topic lead connects with the member, even as he begins
assessing the question, and sets the conditions for effective action.*

If the question isn't aligned with the CC values, the topic lead
connects with the member and talks him through expectations and
perhaps how the question could be rephrased. Similarly, the topic
lead works with the member to clarify the question and to add
context if it is needed. Recall the example of an unclear question
on the previous page. After a topic lead wrote the person who
asked that question, the member rephrased it: "I'm preparing for
command now and am looking for example command philosophies
and, more specifically, how commanders have gone about
communicating their philosophies after taking command." And, of
course, if the question is URGENT, the initial response is to surge
and to provide value to the member in need as quickly as possible.

Regardless of the question, it is excellent if the topic lead can
post an immediate reply online or send a quick email to the person
asking the question, even if it is nothing more than an
acknowledgement that the question has been seen. This response
acts much like a reassuring nod of the head in a face-to-face
conversation. Moreover, it is an opportunity for the topic lead to
establish a connection with the member and to reinforce a sense of
professional community.

Topic leads can also ask their command contacts or other
members they know to respond. Command contacts are a topic
lead's first-response team, and a note to them can generate quick,
effective action: "Team: We've got action. Check out this
question just posted. Please reply and/or forward to someone you
know who has experience in this area."

Moreover, topic leads can do a quick search of the CC member
database, looking for members who have related experience. For
example, Kevin Butler (*Training* topic lead) searched the member
database to find members who listed "convoy ops" in their
experiences and then emailed them asking them to respond to a
question about how to more effectively train convoy operations.

Finally, topic leads can search CC.mil for related discussions
and knowledge objects (content) and then post a reply to the
question, linking the person directly to the relevant content.

Assess and Respond Summary

CC depends on members to participate, both by asking questions and by responding to questions when they have relevant insights. Professional-forum leaders can take action to increase the possibility that the member asking the question gets what he or she needs. For example:

Ensure that the question is clearly stated and provides sufficient detail.

Post an immediate reply online and/or via email to start the conversation and at least to acknowledge to the member that the question has been heard.

Activate command contacts by giving them a heads up about the new question.

Review the online space for existing discussions and/or knowledge objects related to the question and post a reply that links to the relevant content.

Connect with members who have relevant knowledge/experience by searching member dog tags. Ask them to participate in the conversation.

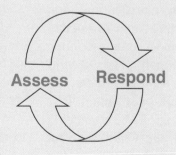

Assess   Respond

What GREAT looks like: When a member posts a question, the community of members blow him away with their response. As a result of the experience, he is a more effective commander, and he has a greater appreciation for the forum as well as for his fellow warriors who *are* the forum.

Close the Loop

Once the question asker has been helped—in other words, once he has asked the question and the community has responded—it is beneficial for him to *close the loop* by posting a comment that describes how he used the information received.

Posting the outcome provides meaningful feedback to the members who took the time to respond to the question. The more specific and detailed the "loop closing" message is, the greater the benefit to those who answered the question. Without such feedback, members who have offered help and advice are left to wonder, *Did the person see it? Was it helpful? Did it matter?*

Once the person has posted a loop-closing message to the discussion, the topic lead can email the members who participated in the discussion to let them know. For example, "Thanks for responding to *so and so*. She just posted a great message that thanks you and tells the "rest of the story" as far as what she did with your input." Writing them ensures that they actually see the message, and it also communicates the topic lead's appreciation.

The practice of closing the loop is also beneficial for the many members who read the discussions, but have not yet asked a question or answered one. When they read a loop-closing message, they see the value being provided to members who ask questions and the impact that members who answer questions can have.

The following post from Allan Barall, serves as a great example of a member taking the time to close the loop:

> I received outstanding insight, clarification, and assistance from several individuals with respect to my post on this unusual situation. Captain Konopa offered great advice. Additionally, I'd like to extend my tremendous thanks for the offline and behind-the-scenes help provided by Captain Ray Kimball and the subject matter experts he connected me with: Captain Rob Barnhill and Chief Warrant Officer Adam Williams. I can't think of another vehicle through which I would have been able to identify problems and possible solutions in a timely manner if not for this Web site. Kudos all around!

Priority Conversations

Instead of good answers, we need good questions. The power of dialogue emerges in the cultivation, in ourselves, as well as in others, of questions for which we do not have answers. Identifying one good question can be vastly more significant than offering many partial answers...look for the really important, hard questions that keep people up nights and go to the heart of our concerns. —William Isaacs[2]

What if topic leads identified or created one powerful question relevant to their topic every other month and then facilitated a productive conversation around it? Doing so would advance their topic and would create amazing value for company commanders. We call these conversations *priority* conversations.

> **W**hat question, if asked in my topic, could generate conversation and deliver significant value to current COs?

The first step in creating a priority conversation is identifying an important issue and then framing it in the form of a question. In some cases, it is a matter of a topic lead choosing a question that a member has already posted. In other cases, topic leads—along with their teams of contacts—identify an important issue and craft a question. We say craft because creating a great question is an art, and we've developed our best questions by vetting them through the team.[3]

> **W**hat is an emerging issue for COs that—if they were talking about it—would make them more effective?

The question may be the catalyst for conversation, but it is the action that a professional-forum leader takes to launch and then to facilitate the conversation that determines its value to members.

> **W**hat question would be worth investing my energy in generating conversation about for two months?

Purpose of a priority conversation: To generate knowledge, to increase company commander effectiveness, and to advance the profession.

Topic Leads: What is your priority conversation right now?

---

[2] William Isaacs, *Dialogue and the Art of Thinking Together*, 1999: p. 148-149.
[3] There are different forms of presenting a question. In addition to asking a question in a discussion area, topic leads also use the *Command Challenges* and *Command Quizzes* to generate priority conversations.

Launch the conversation

Topic leads launch a priority conversation similarly to the description of Deborah launching the MP rally point in Chapter Seven. With a conversation launch, the topic lead and her team identify people they know who have experience relevant to the question (for example, command contacts along with others who have been active in the topic). Topic leads can also search member dog tags to identify members with relevant experience. Moreover, it is helpful to bring in members with diverse viewpoints and wide-ranging experiences whenever possible since diversity of opinion in a conversation helps challenge participants' thinking and broaden perspectives.

The next step is to connect with these members (via email, phone, and through face-to-face connection) and to personally ask them to participate in the conversation (they are pointmen for the conversation). People count it a privilege to be asked to contribute to a specific conversation, especially when the subject is something they are experienced in and passionate about. By asking pointmen to, in turn, invite others to participate, topic leads reach the many through the few.

Additionally, topic leads can feature the question in their online space, send the question out via a survey, and let members know about it via the CC newsletter. These techniques all serve to increase member awareness of the new conversation—without which there simply won't be a conversation.

Finally, depending on the subject area, it may be appropriate to recruit an expert to join the conversation at some point—to perhaps review posted comments and offer his own reflections. For example, in the "Child Dies, Deployment Pending" conversation described in Chapter Four, it might have been helpful to ask the author of a book on death and bereavement to join in the discussion. Because of the time required to do this, it is something for topic leads to consider as they craft the question and then launch the conversation.

In the pages that follow, you will find techniques that have proven effective in helping make the most of online conversations—facilitation techniques that are less about answering a definitive question and more about generating learning, informing judgment, and improving effectiveness. They are techniques for topic leads and facilitators to apply once the conversation has begun.

Facilitate the tone of the conversation

Just as the atmosphere of a physical space influences the conversations within, so too does the tone of an online space. One distinct characteristic of CC.mil is that it is positive and focused on solutions. Members value each other and the knowledge and experience that each bring to the table. This overall quality has been created over time and is reinforced in the way that members communicate with each other. The most powerful way for facilitators to influence tone is in the example that they set. In fact, the way that facilitators interact and communicate is probably the most critical factor influencing tone on CC.mil. Derek Powazek, an experienced online community developer, reinforces how important tone can be:

> If I've learned anything from my years of observing and creating online communities, it's that the tone of the content you give your users is replicated and amplified a thousand times in the responses that it generates. It works almost like an echo: If you scream into a canyon, you'll hear three screams back. If your content is pushy and opinionated you can count on pushy and opinionated responses. If your content is personal and genuine, you'll get personal and genuine responses back. And as the responses grow, that tone is multiplied with each post. A gentle push in one direction can send a fledgling community up to the stars or straight down into the gutter.[4]

Create interaction between participants

As in that best conversation we described earlier, in priority conversations participants build on each other's comments rather than just sequentially stating their own ideas. Facilitators play a key role in making this happen. Three specific techniques follow.

---

[4] Derek M. Powazek, *Design For Community*, 2002: p. 20.

1. Invite a member to build on his comment. The facilitator can build upon or challenge specific thinking, taking the conversation to a deeper level.

> David, I found your comment about providing your operational graphics to the aviation headquarters insightful.   GREAT IDEA!   One thing I'm wondering, given the friction of war, is how do you insure that the pilots flying support actually get the graphics (rather than them staying at HQ)?

In this example, the facilitator addresses the individual involved in the conversation by name, which makes the conversation more personal and also increases the likelihood that he will respond.

2.   Invite other members to build upon a comment.   The facilitator can post a comment in the discussion asking other members to react to something specific that someone posted.   In the process, the facilitator is shaping the conversation and modeling for others the way that one participant might engage another to facilitate learning.   For example:

> Jack raised an important issue. How do others react to his saying "the CDR-1SG relationship is the most important factor influencing a unit's success"?

3. Uncover the reasoning behind comments. In Chapter Four we explained how it is often not the specific position a person takes, but the reasoning that supports his position that helps thinking move forward. The topic lead can solicit this reasoning when it is absent. For example:

> Mary, that is a different view than others have expressed. It would be valuable to understand more about how you got to that view—please lay out your thinking for us.

The way this question is phrased assures Mary that the facilitator believes she has valuable reasoning that would be important to hear, rather than phrasing it as a challenge to her thinking.

Broaden or re-focus the conversation

When a conversation reaches a flex point or loses focus, facilitators broaden the topic or re-focus participants. Five techniques follow.

1. Invite a diversity of opinions. Complete agreement in a conversation may cause members with a different, valuable perspective to remain quiet. In a face-to-face conversation, facial gestures and body language provide good indicators of such disagreement. In a virtual conversation, the facilitator can invite dissenting opinions through a short statement. For example:

> Much of the conversation lately seems to be coming from the same perspective. Is there anyone who has a different way of looking at this issue that would be helpful to us?

In this statement, the facilitator gives assurance that the conversation will be improved by hearing other views.

2. Refocus lagging conversations. When the conversation seems to have lost energy, the facilitator should consider coming at the issue from a new angle. For example:

> We have talked a lot about preparing Soldiers physically for combat. I would like to refocus this discussion to a related topic. Given the amount of time you are going to be deployed, how will you keep your Soldiers fit *during* the deployment?

3. Return to issues that have been bypassed. Sometimes, an issue that has been raised will get lost in the flow of the conversation. If the facilitator believes that the issue could lead to valuable conversation and learning, she can bring it up again. For example:

> Rob raised an issue earlier that we didn't spend much time on—he challenged new commanders to meet one-on-one with every Soldier in the company

within 30 days of assuming command. What are members' reactions to his challenge?

4. Keep the conversation on track. When someone posts a comment that seems tangential, the facilitator can check with that member because often a comment that seems irrelevant or off track will actually contain a perceptive insight that has direct bearing on the current conversation. For example:

> Jim, in your last post you talked about supply discipline. I was having trouble connecting that to counseling your lieutenants, which is what we had been talking about. Could you please share more of your thinking about the connection between supply discipline and lieutenant counseling?

Always giving the participants the benefit of the doubt is one way that facilitators set a learning tone in the conversation.

5. Energize the conversation. In Chapter Four we shared how Chris Engen energized the command challenge discussion of "Child Dies, Deployment Pending" by holding a "live huddle." This was a synchronous conversation scheduled for a one-hour period on a specific day. Compared to the earlier asynchronous conversation, the real-time chat was more spontaneous; people were more responsive to each other, making jokes and voicing their appreciation for what others said. Chris was able to feed some of the insights created in the online huddle into the challenge discussion area, thus invigorating the discussion.

Another great way to energize a conversation is to personally invite new people to join in. An innovative technique is to interview an experienced leader on the subject of the discussion, post the interview directly into the discussion thread, and then invite the interviewee into the discussion as a special guest. For example, to energize a discussion on how to build a great commander-first sergeant team, we interviewed Captain Ryan Morgan and his First Sergeant, Ben Jones. We then posted this interview directly into the discussion thread.

Summarize the conversation

Members are continually learning as they engage in conversations:

- They clarify their own thinking through the act of writing.
- They test their ideas by communicating them and listening to others' responses.
- They change or alter their thinking based on what others have written.
- They become aware of the limitations of their assumptions.

Some of the most useful insights members take away from priority conversations occur when they reflect back on the conversation as a whole. People often find it hard to make sense of an experience or a conversation while they're still in the middle of it. Stepping back allows people to find connections they may have missed in the moment.

A technique that can greatly increase the knowledge generated from an online conversation is to bring it to a close—perhaps after a month or two—and then to create an activity in which the group reflects on what has been learned. One way to do this is to ask everyone who has responded to read back over all the responses and then post a brief paragraph describing what they think the group as a whole has learned—not just themselves as individuals. The facilitator can, of course, draft such a summary on his own, but this approach fails to take advantage of the insights that come to individuals when they create the connections themselves.

Chapter 10

The Afghan Commander Case Study[1]

There is no substitute for experience.   We can more effectively prepare for an experience by connecting with those who have already done what we are preparing to do.

When the company commanders in the 25th Infantry Division's 3rd Brigade Combat Team (Broncos) deployed to Afghanistan in April 2004, they arrived with a powerful intangible weapon: first-hand knowledge and advice from many of their predecessors.   The Bronco leaders were the beneficiaries of a CC team initiative to connect past, present, and future company commanders of the campaign in Afghanistan.   What we call the "Afghan Commander Prep" initiative serves as a fitting summary of the principles and techniques presented throughout this book.

The story begins in October 2003, when Mark Tribus, the Bronco Brigade S-1 and a long-time member of CC, contacted the CC team to ask if we could contribute to the brigade's leader development program.   His unit was six-months away from a one-year deployment to Afghanistan.

---

[1] This chapter is a testament to the Army profession and to leaders like Major Mark Tribus, who was the catalyst for this initiative. Everything he does is first class, and we count it a privilege to call him a team member and friend.

In responding to this opportunity, we used the same process that topic leads use to develop their respective topics. In fact, it's the same process we used to launch CompanyCommand.army.mil:

- Set Direction (Purpose, Vision, Values)
- Identify Priorities
- Develop a Strategy
- Build the Team
- Develop Content
- Facilitate Conversations
- Create Connections

First Steps

After numerous discussions with Bronco Brigade leaders during October and November, we settled on a purpose: to improve the 3rd Brigade Combat Team company commanders' effectiveness in Afghanistan. But after these initial conversations, we didn't know enough to be able to establish the program's priorities up front. They would have to emerge from the input provided by those who actually knew what was most important: experienced Afghan commanders and Bronco Brigade leaders. The priorities that eventually rose to the top of the list were: warfighting, convoy operations, intelligence development at the company level, communications, rear detachment operations, understanding the Afghan culture, and Family Readiness Group leadership.

Our strategy—shaped by purpose, our initial sense of priorities, and a realistic assessment of our resources—consisted of four distinct projects:

Creating the *Afghan Commander AAR Book*

After surveying the experienced Afghan commanders, we collated their responses into a book and delivered it to the commanders preparing for Afghanistan. The first draft, which included the responses of 25 commanders, was delivered in January 2004; an updated book with input from 41 commanders was published in

March.[2] (The quotations from commanders like Captain Ryan Worthan highlighted throughout this chapter are excerpts from the *Afghan Commander AAR Book*.)

> *You will only be there when it starts about 1 in 5 times, so your personal leadership is NOT the most important thing. You have to develop the trust and confidence in your SLs, PSGs, and PLs to do what is right. Once you leave the wire, there is no turning back and no second chances. If your leaders know that they have your trust, they will not hesitate...and they will win.*
> —**Ryan Worthan, A/1-87 IN, OEF 4**

Sponsoring a pro-reading program

In January 2004, we sent every Bronco Brigade commander copies of the book *Taliban*. (Implementation of this reading program by Todd Schmidt is highlighted in Chapter 3, "Talking About Books.")

Facilitating an Afghan leader-to-leader (L2L) workshop

The L2L workshops were a large-scale implementation of the *Hubbard Effect* described in Chapter Two. In March 2004, six experienced Afghan commanders and two experienced FRG leaders met for three days with Bronco Brigade leaders.

Launching the Afghan commander forum

We decided to create a virtual community where past, present, and future Afghan commanders could share their Afghan-related tools, experiences, and ideas. In February 2004, this forum was launched within CompanyCommand.army.mil.

*****

The first step in building the Afghan commander prep team involved creating a "who's who" map (NETMAP) of company commanders who had served in Afghanistan, organized by OEF rotation. By calling division G3 offices, contacting deployed units, and asking friends for help, we were able to track down commanders who had served with the 101st Airborne Division, the 10th Mountain Division, and the 82nd Airborne Division in Afghanistan.

We wrote or called these leaders, explaining our vision and requesting their participation in an AAR survey. Forty-one leaders

---

[2] Captain Rob Griggs flew to Hawaii and, with Mark Tribus, hand-delivered the initial copies of the book in January. Rob's visit reinforced the CC team's relationship with the 3rd BCT leaders and was instrumental in understanding how to subsequently provide the most value.

completed the survey, including 13 commanders who were on the ground in Afghanistan.

Email Sent to all Afghan-Experienced Commanders

On behalf of the http://CompanyCommand.army.mil team, I'm writing to request your help with a HUGE project we've taken on in support of our comrades who are preparing to head to Afghanistan now. We are working in partnership with the Third Brigade 25th ID to help them prepare for combat. As part of this effort, we are capturing the input of officers who have commanded at the company level in AFG, using a web-based AAR designed specifically for this purpose. **[CLICK HERE]** to complete the survey.

Would you take the time to do this?

We will personally hand deliver the booklets to the 25th ID commanders who are getting ready now. The real-time and relevant contribution of guys like you will be HUGE and will make an immediate and very significant impact on our comrades getting ready for combat now.

Thanks for being willing to consider this. We envision this initiative having incredible impact on the effectiveness of our leaders' preparation and on our ability to generate key learnings. This won't happen without your help.

You are really all on your own out there. We were over 10 kilometers (and 4000 feet) from any other friendly unit, and when we had Soldiers who became cold weather casualties, the only thing that saved them was what we could do for them ourselves. Nobody was coming for them. There were no trucks and MEDEVAC was unable to fly. PCIs/PCCs are critical so that you ensure you have all the necessary tools to react to the major contingencies that may come up.
—*Chris Nyland, C/2-504 PIR, OEF 3*

After asking every Afghan-experienced commander we could find for help with the survey, we recruited a more focused group to conduct the L2L workshop with Bronco Brigade leaders.[3]

---

[3] The team that came together and traveled to the 25th Infantry Division consisted of: Kevin Butler (Infantry), Eric Lopez (Infantry), John Miller (Infantry), Mario Ochoa (Aviation), Lance Curtis (Quartermaster and a recent Rear Detachment Cdr), Mike Martel (Signal), Christy Lopez (FRG Leader), and Traci Cook (FRG Leader).

Making It Happen

Every element of the Afghan commander prep strategy was designed to foster connections, conversations, and the creation of valuable content. The AAR book, for example, relied on connections to create content—and the content led to conversations and more connections. The pro-reading program used a great piece of content to create conversations. The leader-to-leader workshop facilitated conversations and generated new connections. And the online forum serves as a place where leaders can post content, engage in conversations, and connect with each other. More detailed descriptions of the *Afghan Commander AAR Book* and the L2L workshop follow, since they were such crucial elements of the overall program.

> *The defining moment for me was the first time we operated in the mountains. You hear how rugged the terrain is, but you really cannot appreciate it until you are there. Ensure that you have a very challenging PT program as we have covered 67 km in five days on one operation and 52 km in 4 days in another.*
> —**Toby Moore, B/2-22 IN, OEF 4**

The AAR book

The *Afghan Commander AAR Book*'s purpose was to provide valuable company-level content to the leaders of the Bronco Brigade. We also envisioned it being a starting point for valuable conversations within the Bronco Brigade. Above all, we wanted to provide a variety of perspectives—not just pat answers—that, by informing commanders' judgment, would enable them to make better combat decisions.

Most of the book's content came from the online survey, in which we asked respondents to imagine that they were in a conversation with fellow commanders who were preparing to deploy. This helped create an informal tone, which, combined with the respondents' earthy descriptions and attention to detail, produced a document that the Bronco Brigade leaders found appealing and accessible.

The following response serves as an example of what we mean. Instead of just writing "Bring Goretex Bellevue desert boots," in response to the second survey question—"What piece of gear/equipment made the most difference for you personally while you were in Afghanistan?"—Dwight Phillips gave an answer that helped cement his advice in readers' minds:

Goretex "Bellevue" desert boots. An infantry Soldier is going to walk in some rough terrain here. Without good boots, you are in trouble. I waded through glacial rivers in the mountains without getting my feet wet. These boots held up well in sub-freezing temps.

Moreover, at the end of each section in the book, we added information about the participating commanders, including their contact information. This enabled leaders who were preparing for Afghanistan to continue the conversation with experienced commanders after the workshop.

Afghan Commander AAR Questions

1. If a CO could read only one book on AFG before deploying, what book should they read, and why?

2. What piece of gear/equipment made the most difference for you personally while in Afghanistan? For your Soldiers?

3. What collective tasks did your unit perform the most while in Afghanistan? In other words, what types of missions did you get called on to perform most often?

4. If a Soldier is going to get hurt in Afghanistan (not battle related), how is it most likely going to happen? What could a future Afghan CO do to help prevent it?

5. What is one thing that surprised you when you got to Afghanistan? Explain.

6. Describe one or two innovations you implemented and how they made a difference—for example, tactical innovations, modifications to equipment, doctrine, or how you planned and/or organized for missions.

7. What was the defining moment/experience for you in Afghanistan? That is, what experience stands out the most for you?

Afghan Commander AAR Questions (cont)

8. If you were preparing to deploy to Afghanistan again, what is one thing you would focus more on than you did, and why?

9. What is one thing you spent time on during preparation that didn't apply in country?

10. Did the weather/terrain impact your operations? Describe an experience you had where weather/terrain impacted you.

11. Which one or two of the following concerns affected you the most in Afghanistan: resupply, communication, transportation, maintenance, or convoy ops? Please select and then explain your choice(s).

12. Which one or two of the following issues affected you the most in Afghanistan: intelligence, local Afghan leaders, translators, coalition partners, or NGOs? Please select and then explain your choice(s).

13. Of the following topics, which one or two affected you the most in Afghanistan: physical fitness, marksmanship, mental fitness, combat lifesaver/medical, or spiritual fitness? Please select and then explain your choice(s).

14. What would you tell a 25th ID commander about FRGs and/or Soldier morale that might help him/her prepare?

15. What experience could you pass on about dealing with U.S. casualties that might help a commander who is preparing to deploy to Afghanistan?

16. Is there anything else that you would like to pass on to your comrades preparing to deploy to Afghanistan now?

The L2L workshop

In March 2004, six U.S. Army officers who had recently commanded companies in Afghanistan and two experienced FRG leaders visited with the Bronco Brigade leaders for a three-day L2L workshop. The face-to-face connections and conversations that occurred during this time helped make the content that was delivered really hit home.

Our team arrived early to meet with the brigade's leadership team, finalize the schedule of events, and ensure that the implementation of the plan was consistent with the unit's needs. The day before the event, the L2L team conducted a review of the CC team's vision, values, and purpose. We also rehearsed our presentations twice to ensure that we were communicating our stories with enough passion and detail to make the lessons come alive.

L2L Day 1: Kick-off luncheon and informal sharing. Fifty-three leaders from the Bronco Brigade Combat Team attended the L2L luncheon, which was sponsored by AUSA Hawaii, and listened as the team shared key experiences. (Attendees sat by unit at round tables; a member of the L2L team was at each table.) Each of the seasoned Afghan commanders shared three focused stories that captured a key learning: one from pre-deployment, one from when the unit was operating in Afghanistan, and one from post-deployment. Eric Lopez set the stage with his introduction:

> One month ago my company was ambushed in Afghanistan. In fact, we were ambushed on the same road that you will be using as you work in and out of your firebase. Two of my guys were wounded as we fought our way out. We learned some valuable lessons through spilt blood and sweat. And I'm here to share these lessons with you so that you can hit the ground running and continue the mission.

Their stories brought the lessons learned to life. For example, instead of simply saying, "Make sure your Soldiers' family-contact information is up to date," one leader went into detail sharing, "Our unit spent three weeks trying to find a spouse whose husband was wounded and in the hospital. She had gone home to spend time with a friend and had not notified anyone."

After the luncheon, each team member linked up with a sponsoring battalion for the rest of the afternoon while FRG leaders Traci Cook and Christy Lopez facilitated an informal session with the Bronco Brigade's FRG leaders. That evening, an informal social provided more opportunities for Afghan commanders past and future to talk about the challenges of leadership in Afghanistan.

L2L Day 2: Leaders at sponsoring units. Since the sponsoring units knew which formats and opportunities for interaction would be most valuable for their team, they determined the structure for the second day. The result, in some cases, was that the Afghanistan veterans met with large groups—from squad leaders on up. In other cases, the veterans spent one-on-one time with company commanders, going to each company in sequence. These sessions enabled the veterans to go over maps, review plans, and address the specific questions and concerns of the commanders who were preparing to deploy. In many instances, participants found the informal sessions more valuable than the structured briefings—further testimony that these more casual opportunities for interaction are too important to be left to chance.

> *If you have casualties, then get an update about those casualties for your Soldiers. It is important to them to know that their buddies are being taken care of because they feel that they could be next. As an example here in Iraq, we had a Soldier who was hit in the leg with an RPG; he subsequently lost his leg. Other Soldiers were happy to hear that he had received a $100,000 prosthetic leg from Walter Reed Army Hospital. If you have any Soldiers die, it is important to recognize them with a memorial service. This helps those who miss him and fear their own mortality.*
> *—Bret Tecklenburg, B/2-187 IN, OEF 1*

L2L Day 3: Working seminars. On the third day, the team facilitated four concurrent seminars related to the event's main priorities: convoy operations, rear-detachment, company-level intelligence, and communications. The breadth of experience in the team was especially apparent at the rear-detachment seminar, which included a commander who had just redeployed (Eric Lopez), his unit's family-readiness group leader (Christy Lopez), a recent rear-detachment commander at Ft. Campbell (Lance Curtis), and an experienced FRG leader (Traci Cook). Every rear detachment commander for the Bronco Brigade attended; participants gained first-hand insight into how forward-deployed commanders, rear-detachment commanders, and family-readiness group leaders can work together effectively.

Assessing the Impact

Immediately following the leader-to-leader workshops in Hawaii, we received overwhelmingly positive feedback from the 3rd BCT leaders. For example, Lieutenant Colonel Walt Piatt, commander of Task Force 2-27 IN, noted that the *Afghan Commander AAR Book* was the best he'd ever read. "We adjusted our training plan based on it," he said. However, the real proof of the value provided by this initiative came from the company commanders once they were on the ground in Afghanistan conducting combat operations. Seven months into the operation, company commanders in the 3rd BCT were asked, "What document, AAR, book, or conversation assisted you the most in your pre-deployment training?" Several responses speak to the impact of the Afghan Commander Prep initiative:

> Talking with the company commanders who had already been in Afghanistan, especially those who had recently been in Afghanistan.
> —Chris Owen, B/2-5 IN

> Meetings with company commanders who had OEF experience. It was invaluable conducting a face-to-face with someone who was there. The book *Taliban*, by Rashid, was the most informative piece of literature because it provided the reader with a sense of the social, political, and economic situation in Afghanistan. It gave the reader a sense of what to expect and look for when you got on the ground.
> —Gyles Gregory, HHC/2-5 IN

> A company commander [Eric Lopez] from the unit we were replacing came to our home station and briefed unit leaders on his experiences and TTPs learned in theatre. His briefing helped prioritize local training and alleviate some concern about what to expect once arrived. Also, the CompanyCommand AAR book.
> —John Sego, B/2-27 IN

The CompanyCommand AAR book. Why? It was the most relevant as it discussed real world scenarios and what to expect.
                        —Tage Rainsford, C/2-27 IN

I think the most important document, AAR, book, or conversation that assisted us in our pre-deployment training and focus was speaking with the company commanders that had commanded in Afghanistan.   —Rick Smith, B/3-7 FA

After the event in Hawaii, we followed up with each of the 41 officers who contributed to the *Afghan Commander AAR Book*. We mailed them a copy of the AAR book, a CompanyCommand baseball cap, and a letter of thanks, which included comments of appreciation from the leaders in the 25th ID(L) and an invitation to continue the conversation via the *Afghan Commander* topic on CC.mil. We close this chapter by again thanking these contributors. We are in awe of their desire to make a difference for the company commanders in the 25th ID(L). In the process, they have made a difference for the entire profession.

*****

The story of the Afghan Commander Prep initiative enables the fundamental insight we've emphasized throughout this book—conversation, connections, and relevant content are the lifeblood of a vibrant professional forum—to be seen in high relief. Participating in this event was a capstone experience for our team. Not only did it give us an opportunity to bring together much of what we had learned over the past four years, but the work of putting the pieces together to present to others added a depth and dimension to our own understanding. It is our earnest hope that as you apply the frameworks and practices we've shared, your experiences will be similar.

Hall of Honor

Captain Michael Tarlavsky (Commander, ODA 512) was killed living out the motto of "Follow Me!" during combat operations in Najaf, Iraq on 12 August 2004. Mike's exceptional contributions to the *Afghan Commander AAR Book* serve as an example of one warrior passing on what he was learning to those who follow in his footsteps. It is especially awe-inspiring to know that Mike led an SF team in Afghanistan (OEF 1) as part of the initial entry and destruction of the  Taliban regime, and he was on his second combat deployment to Iraq when he made the ultimate sacrifice. Mike is further honored in the *Hall of Honor* section of CompanyCommand.army.mil.

PART 3

Chapter 11

Mentor Symposium

...Etienne Wenger, Kent Greenes, Hubert Saint-Onge

Our efforts to support company-level leaders through professional forums have benefited greatly from the insights of others. Just as we encourage company commanders to connect with each other in conversation, so too have we sought out and benefited greatly from leaders who have experience and insights into the work that professional forum leaders do. We believe that our ability to deliver world-class value to company commanders is tightly connected to our willingness to learn from others in this way. Three legendary leaders in the fields of knowledge management and learning that we have had the privilege of being connected with for the last couple of years include Etienne Wenger, Kent Greenes, and Hubert Saint-Onge. They have had a big impact on us, so we are extremely excited to have them share some of their experience and wisdom with you here.

Our intent is for you to experience what we have experienced—Etienne, Kent, and Hubert speaking to you in their own voices. Each offers his own perspective, based on his particular approach, experiences, and interests. Etienne is a brilliant theoretician, Kent is an unparalleled practitioner, and Hubert is a renowned practitioner who develops theoretical models in his recent books. Yet, their advice is remarkably consistent, weaving together like strands of twine to provide a strong vision of what professional forums need to survive and thrive.

We asked each of them the same question:

**"What advice do you have for someone serving in the role of
a professional forum leader?"**

Etienne Wenger

Etienne Wenger has spent his life studying learning systems, driven by the basic idea that people learn together and knowledge is situated in community. Along with his colleague Jean Lave, he is known for having coined the term communities of practice. His books have been incredibly helpful to us and have provided us a theoretical perspective and language to better understand and describe our work with professional forums. We connected with Etienne personally in 2002 and have stayed in touch with him ever since. In our conversations, Etienne always wants to know more about what we are doing with CompanyCommand—always asking and listening more than he talks. Yet, without exception, we come away from those conversations with new insights and challenges. The more we learn, the more we come to value the depth of Etienne's wisdom, and the more we appreciate his mentorship.

"When cultivating communities in organizations, it is important for leaders to keep in mind what communities are about, what gives them life. The main difference between a community and a hierarchical structure is that a community fundamentally works on identity. It is a place of engagement of the self, a place of heart. This is so because for true professionals, learning is not merely a technical issue; it is a *way of realizing who they are.* You must understand that a community is a place where you can be who you are as a professional, and where you enable others to find their voices and be who they are. You build community when *who you are* touches *who someone else is.* That identification—that process of two learners connecting—is very powerful.

"This presents challenges for community leaders and for organizational leaders.

"For community leaders, the key challenge is to *make it personal.* Your best resource is who you are. Although this book describes many excellent techniques that can help build community, community-building itself is not a technique. The CompanyCommand people have been able to accomplish what they have because they come from a place of passion and a place of identity. They have great passion for company command and a very strong identity as military leaders. Community leaders have to create a sense of belonging among their members, and that sense can come only from their own sense of belonging. You can't help build identity in others unless you possess it yourself. Again, the best resource you have to generate value and build community is *who you are.*

"This is not to say that the technical aspects of design and procedure are unimportant. We know that some techniques are important to community development—rules of thumb like don't overwhelm people with content, organize content in a way people can relate to, mix pull and push of information, develop a rhythm of community activities, and many others. But these techniques can only *support, not replace*, the passion and identity that are so important in leaders of a professional forum.

"On a more practical note, I encourage all community leaders to stay in touch with each other. First of all, it lets you know the latest thinking. Second, it nurtures your identity as a topic leader. It helps you grow into that way of being.

"I also want to advise community leaders never to underestimate 'back-stage' work. It's easy to think as a leader that your responsibility is the 'front-page' stuff—the content, the conversations, the things that are visible. But in fact it's the back-stage work—keeping in touch, calling people, knowing people—that is so important to building a successful community. Back-stage work leads to front-page results. That is why you need the passion. Back-stage work doesn't get noticed or produce immediate results; you will do it only if that is who you are and what you are passionate about.

"It is an exciting time to be a community leader because you are contributing to a reinvention of the organization.

"For organizations, the great challenge in the next decade is to figure out how communities and formal structures can work together most effectively. Despite the misgivings of some organizational leaders, community does not compete with hierarchy. Both must exist in an organization, and they don't subsume each other. They are two sides of the same learning coin, complementing each other to build a knowledge organization. Communities generate learning, and hierarchies put that learning to work to accomplish organizational goals. They work differently, yet are essential to each other's success.

"The challenge for the Army, and for all organizations, is to figure out how to institutionalize the fact of communities without institutionalizing communities. There's a big difference. Institutionalizing the fact of communities within an organization means providing them sponsorship, resources, and recognition, as well as listening to their suggestions. On the other hand, institutionalizing communities means absorbing them into the bureaucracy—and that is fatal to communities!

"Figuring out how to support and integrate communities in organizations without inadvertently killing them is not an easy task. We have made progress. Today there are lots of examples of organizations in the private and public sectors where communities play an important role. But there is still a lot to learn. There is an enormous source of value creation in the conversations people have, in engaging their identity with a problem, in thinking for themselves, not just doing what they're told. So, you have to bring that source above ground so it can actually deliver that value. You have to integrate the value of communities into how you understand the value-creation processes of the organization. But there lies a danger, and the great danger is that you forget what makes the community work, what makes it tick, and all of a sudden the form has replaced the function, and the community withers.

"It's like the story of the goose that laid the golden egg. People wanted the gold, so they went right in and cut up the goose, only to discover that there was no gold inside. Their rush to gather immediate gold ruined their opportunity to benefit from years of golden eggs. It is the same with organizations and communities. Communities will provide great value to an organization, but the hierarchy must let them live. As organizational and community leaders, you 'feed the goose.' You nurture a system that produces what only it can produce. And that knowledge, that learning, that sense of identity among professionals within the organization—is as good as gold.

"I close by returning to my main points, which I think are so important. Organizational leaders, understand both the organizational value and the personal nature of community. Community leaders, use your selves as a source of value and a source of creation. Use your own person, passion, and identity as your main vehicle to build community. If you want to unleash the power of professionalism, don't substitute for it. Keep focused on people, not procedures; on relationships, not rules; and recognize that the journey you are traveling is uncharted, but your passion and identity have proven true thus far, so let them continue to guide you."

Kent Greenes

Kent Greenes is one of the world's most respected leaders in the knowledge-management field today. When he gives advice, it is grounded in over two decades of practical, in-the-arena work helping people increase their effectiveness. Before SAIC, his current company, Kent was a key leader for British Petroleum (BP) where his work ranged from leading AARs on an off-shore oil platform to implementing a virtual teamwork program that allowed knowledge sharing to occur across the entire organization. His work impacted BP to the tune of $260 million in 1998 alone! Over the last couple of years, he has been a fantastic coach for our team. Typically, he will listen intently to us and then will ask a probing question—the kind that you keep turning over in your mind for weeks after. He is never shy about telling us when he thinks we have it "all wrong" and is just as eager to encourage and share his experience with us. Having his support is like having the wind at your back.

"I'm going to direct my comments to those who are thinking of starting a community or forum, whatever you choose to call it, in their organization. I've seen a lot of communities—in the corporate world, in non-profit organizations, in government—and about half succeed and half fail. I have, however, noticed what seem to be characteristics that lead consistently to success or failure. I hope that these comments help.

"First, if you are thinking of starting a community, ask yourself if you feel a real need for one. If there's not a need, a knowledge gap, a sense that 'we can do this better,' then it will be very hard for a community to gain traction. If the reason you are starting a community is only because it sounds like a good idea, or because everyone else is doing it, or because the boss said so—and not because it's the best way to meet a genuine need—then that's a problem. I recommend that you not waste your time.

"If there is a real need for a community, then it is essential that the right people take the lead. Community leaders must have passion for what they're doing—passion for the subject area and for the people who are a part of it. I think that passion is so important that I now refer to communities of practice as 'communities of passion,' because they simply don't succeed without it. Building and sustaining communities for the long haul take so much effort that passion seems to be the only fuel that can sustain them. Therefore, it is very important that the right kind of people—passionate people—are the leaders of communities.

"Community leaders must also have an ethic of service. Ask yourself, 'Do I want to help others be as successful as they can be?' If you don't, you won't be willing to share your hard-earned insights and knowledge, and you won't go the extra mile to do the things that a community requires. Communities don't just happen by themselves. They require passionate leadership that willingly serves the members. Anything less isn't worth doing.

"Okay, so you feel a real need in your subject area, and you are passionately committed to addressing the problem by building community. What next? Start by talking to your professional peers and colleagues about your plans. This does several things. One, it validates that the problem is real. It also begins to build competence, generate enthusiasm, and allow a critical mass of networks to grow. A community is built on relationships. The relationships that provide the initial energy for a professional community are those that radiate from its leaders.

"I know that sometimes communities are launched with a top-down, big-splash approach, but I don't see that working very often. The most successful communities I see are those that develop bottom-up or middle-out, because then the members are more likely to have ownership of it and its success.

"Now, even if it starts totally grass roots, every community—if it is successful—will evolve to a point where it needs sponsorship from the organization. Depending on the culture of the organization, it may be smart to get that sponsorship up front, if for no other reason than to assure potential members that the organization does not disapprove of their participation. As long as the community is aligned with the strategic goals of the organization—which it should be—then organizational leaders will likely give their support and approval. Still, at some point, participation in the community will involve so much attention and time from employees that someone in the organization's hierarchy will demand that it justify itself. At this time, it will be nice to have a sponsor, although the ultimate and only meaningful justification will be the testimonies of the members themselves. If their community has indeed provided them value, then they should be willing to speak up and say how it has helped them do their job. If members are not willing to speak up, then perhaps the community is not worth the effort it is requiring.

"The experience of CompanyCommand follows the pattern I describe. The people who started it felt a strong need to address a problem that really bothered them—there was no efficient way for commanders to share their key insights with each other and with the next generation of commanders. They were passionate about doing something about it, and they leveraged in a powerful way their social network to build and sustain the community. They started bottom up, but they intentionally shared their vision with some senior Army leaders they had relationships with to secure implicit sponsorship. At one point, a senior officer in their rating chain demanded that they justify the time and energy they were dedicating to their unofficial effort; they asked the community for words of support, and within three days they received twenty-five pages worth of testimony. Now they have evolved to having official sponsorship and support from the Army. This experience isn't unique to CompanyCommand. It is a pattern I see in many successful communities as they grow and evolve.

"I said earlier that communities are built on relationships, and I'd like to go into that a little deeper. Especially with online communities, we can see the content and conversations, and it's easy to overlook how that content and conversation came about, and how it can lead to usable knowledge. It all starts with relationships. Relationships are built over time by people getting together and having conversations, and those relationships generate trust. Trust is really important. Trust leads people to share their knowledge and insights. In most cases, our knowledge involves what I call 'half don't knows,' in which we possess knowledge that is significant and relevant to us, but we're not sure if it would be relevant or applicable to others. If we share it, we might sound stupid. In an environment of trust, people are willing to share their 'half don't knows.' They are willing to express their views because they trust that they won't be made to feel stupid.

"Relationships also facilitate the most powerful kind of knowledge transfer, that which passes directly from one person's brain into another's, in a conversation where context can be communicated though the back-and-forth exchange. Knowledge that is codified into content—written down or put on media— before it is shared is transferred less effectively. Granted, if people have contexts and experiences very similar to those of the contributor of a piece of content, they may be able to use the content 'as is,' but more commonly they can make use of only some of it. The unfortunate fact is, as soon as you codify content, it loses some of its meaning. Therefore, conversation is the most powerful way to transfer knowledge.

"An idea that emerged earlier this year in a conversation I had with the CompanyCommand team is that conversation, content, and context need to be tightly coupled and integrated. They feed off of each other. You create content from meaningful conversation. Content attracts more people. The people engage in more conversation, often about existing content, generating more context and new content. The most powerful use of content is to spark more informed conversations, because that is what gets people actually transferring knowledge so they can use it right now.

"The Afghan peer assist project is a great example of how relationships can lead to content that sparks valuable conversation. The CompanyCommand folks used their relationships with commanders who had served in Afghanistan to generate content, the AAR book. Then, they set up face-to-face conversations among past and future Afghan commanders, and those conversations were informed by the content of the AAR book. In the course of those conversations, new relationships formed, and people developed the trust necessary to bring up knowledge that could sound stupid, like, 'Hey, have you ordered mouse traps? The tents in Afghanistan attract rats, and rats attract vipers, and you don't want vipers in your tents, so you need lots of mousetraps to keep the rats away.' Who would have thought that companies in Afghanistan need mousetraps? Not the commanders who had not yet been there. That important piece of knowledge emerged only from the interplay of relationships, trust, content, conversation, and context.

"If you are a community leader, an understanding of the interplay between conversation, content, and context can help you put energy and effort into the right things. It's an integrated, holistic way of looking at community-building. Good luck to you. What you are doing is so important to the Army and our country that I feel honored to be able to contribute."

Hubert Saint-Onge

We first learned about Hubert Saint-Onge by reading his book, Leveraging Communities of Practice for Strategic Advantage. *The book describes his work creating and launching a learning community that laterally connected 3,000 independent insurance agents spread across Canada. The book is full of lessons learned and practical insights that apply directly to our work with professional forums—it was exciting to read! We have since met Hubert and count it a privilege to call him a mentor and a friend. When you hear Hubert talk, the thing that strikes you is how passionate he is about helping people be more effective in their work. His energy and desire to make a difference is infectious—to the point that when you walk away from a conversation with him, you want to go out and conquer the world.*

"The first and foremost role of a community leader is to contribute to the empowerment of the members of the community. Community leaders are there at the service of the knowledge domain and the other members of the community.

"Community leaders *put oxygen into the system* to keep it humming. They ask questions to start discussions, ask questions within discussions to bring out key learning points, ask questions to get to know the members better. In my opinion, topic leaders should spend 90% of their time asking questions, and 10% answering them. Remember, the knowledge is there in the individual members; the leaders just have to help draw it out so it can be shared.

"As an online community leader, you want to create an environment within the desktop where *people recognize themselves*, because that's what engenders trust. It's great that CompanyCommand indicates 'who's online' and you can see those members' profiles. It's important that members see that the community is a place for people like them. Having photos of members, names and units attached to content—all of this helps members relate to other members and feel a part of the community.

"One of the great sources of motivation for community members is when they see that they are *building a knowledge domain*. When topic leads convert a discussion's main learning points into content, when they create new knowledge objects from conversations or other knowledge objects, they are building the expertise of the community. The community can then have conversations about that new knowledge object, and the knowledge grows even more, it moves forward. When members see this sort of knowledge-building progress, and especially when they have been able to contribute to that progress, they become very motivated. They take pride in building their profession's knowledge domain. So, it is important that community leaders develop this sense of communal knowledge building.

"Now, you have to be careful how you do it. The community itself must build the knowledge. Keep the voices of the contributors. Keep the richness of the language. Cut and paste, don't summarize. *Extract, don't abstract.* In my opinion, 90% of all lessons-learned efforts in organizations are useless, because the knowledge is extracted by someone who doesn't understand the knowledge domain, organized into a taxonomy that doesn't make sense, and delivered as abstract bullets. It is important to keep the voice, the context, and the richness that make the information usable within the domain.

"One of the dangers of having strong and active topic leads is that they inadvertently create the sense that they own the knowledge, that they own the domain. It is essential that, while they take responsibility for their domain, topic leads keep in mind that they are *custodians, not owners*, of the domains. I want topic leads to create leadership within the community that is more disparate than themselves. I want them to be distributors of leadership, and distributors of a sense of ownership for what the community does. All members of a professional community are owners of their knowledge domain. All are responsible for building the knowledge domain. All must understand that the process of conversation is a productive process, one that leads to new knowledge. If topic leads can create this sense of shared responsibility, there is no limit to the learning and knowledge building that will occur.

"Most people who join a community do so to find information. The challenge for community leaders is to get members to evolve to the sense that, 'I am here because my voice counts, my ideas are here and valued, and I am contributing to the knowledge domain.' When members take ownership, communities thrive. Conversely, a sure sign of what I call undue institutionalization of a community is when someone from outside it is approving its content. That is the kiss of death. Community members must take responsibility for their own domain, and then they will take pride in it.

"CompanyCommand is the best example of its kind that I have seen anywhere in the world, but there is room for improvement in the areas I have addressed. It is great to have a team of 30 topic leads who feel a strong sense of ownership, but having 300 or 3000 members who feel fully invested in building the knowledge domain would be even better! Conversations are great, but the team could do better at building content from them, which I know they are trying to do.

"Two final points. One, if you are a topic lead within a community, remember that you serve the community as a whole, not just your own topic. Always be thinking how you can share your topic's content and conversations across the community. Cross-fertilize knowledge.

"Two, remember that there is an ethic that community leaders must espouse. Communities are not just about information; the information has to be dressed in the right ethics and values. People have to know and trust each other. Integrity of leadership is absolutely essential. Communities thrive in the 'passionate zone,' not the 'bureaucratic zone.' Keep the passion, spread the passion, and your community's knowledge building can make a great impact."

*****

Afterword

Third-Generation Leadership

...*Leaving a legacy*

> I am an American Soldier. I am a Warrior and a member of a team. I serve the people of the United States and live the Army Values...I am an expert, and I am a professional...–from *The Soldier's Creed*

One of the main ideas of this book is that connecting leaders in conversation about their work transforms the individuals who participate as well as the whole of the profession. To be effective individually and collectively, members of the profession must have access to each other and to the knowledge that they develop together.

While professional forums are helping to unleash the power of the Army profession, the source of that power is the warrior ethos and foundational values that define the Army—its "DNA." And it is through the practice of developing leaders that this ethos is passed on from one generation to the next. In this way, the profession is continuously in the process of producing its own future.

Third-Generation Leadership and Leader Development

Before thinking about the future, we need to think about the past. Think about one person who has significantly influenced your development as a leader. (Picture this person in your mind....)

For Steve Delvaux, that person was Captain Hank Arnold, Steve's company commander when he was a lieutenant in C/5-502nd (Berlin Brigade). During the Captain's Career Course, we had the privilege of hearing newly promoted Captain Delvaux tell story after story about Captain Arnold and the example that he set developing his lieutenants. In fact, we affectionately began calling them "Hank" stories and could recount them as if they were our own. Steve went on to command a rifle company in the 101st where Hank's imprint could be seen in the way Steve developed his own lieutenants. Hank Arnold's legacy is the leaders that he influenced and—more powerfully—the leaders that his leaders are influencing today and into the future.

The Hank Arnold/Steve Delvaux story is an excellent example of third-generation leadership.[1] This is the idea that the investment you make in developing your Soldiers will decidedly influence successive generations.

Parenting provides a useful illustration of this concept in action. A third-generation perspective on parenting involves raising kids with your grandchildren in mind. In the process, you explain what you are doing and pass on a developmental vision so that your kids are inspired and equipped to do the same with their children. The rewards of parenting in this way are delayed; in fact, the full impact is often never seen by the parent.

This is true for leadership as well. Leaders with a third-generation perspective develop their leaders with future generations in mind. While they influence primarily by role modeling *how* to lead, they also impart the *why* behind their actions in such a way that their Soldiers are not only inspired, but are also equipped to do the same with their subordinate leaders. For example, a company commander might ask a platoon leader to describe what she is doing to develop her squad leaders with the additional expectation that she do the same thing with them. She would then ask each squad leader to describe how they are developing their team leaders. In this process, the company commander is role modeling by developing the platoon leader, and he is not leaving the further application to chance. By having the platoon leader lay out how she is developing her squad leaders, the

---

[1] Our team first heard about this third-generation perspective on leadership from Dan Wooldridge, who is our respected colleague and mentor in the area of leader development.

commander is putting third-generation leadership into motion. Success is not developing great leaders. Rather, success is developing great leaders who themselves have a personal vision to develop great leaders.

The power of example, combined with understanding the why behind it, is a potent force for influencing the way that leaders lead. For example, in Chapter 3, "Talking About Books," we described how George Corbari inscribed a personal note inside each book that he gave to his leaders. Asked why he did this, George cited the memorable experience of having his own company commander do the same for him years earlier.

The impact of leader development is largely delayed, so leaders are often unaware of the influence they are having. George Corbari's company commander has no idea that George carried on many of the things he did. Likewise, George probably won't see the impact of his actions in the lives of the leaders he is developing, but he knows it is making a difference because he experienced that difference in his own life.

Generalized reciprocity is a term that describes this process: you invest in someone—not because you expect an immediate return from the person (i.e., direct reciprocation)—but because you have been developed by others. It is a vision passed on from one generation to the next. This is a powerful principle to have at work in an organization, especially in one like the Army in which all leaders must be developed from within.

Third-Generation Leadership and Advancing the Profession

A third-generation mindset opens up possibilities—possibilities that extend beyond leader development and expand how we think about our role within the profession. Colonel Don Snider and Gayle Watkins recently led a research project that studied the current state of the Army profession. In their book, they write:

> Expertise and the knowledge underlying it are the coins of the professional realm. More so than other occupations and organizations, professions focus on

generating expert knowledge and the ability of its members to apply that expertise to new situations.[2]

The nature of a military profession—a sense of calling, deep commitment, shared values, corporate cohesion, and loyalty—creates the conditions for knowledge to be seen as a corporate asset which should be developed and shared as a condition of being a member.[3] Creating expert knowledge, sharing and teaching it to each other, and applying it must be woven into the very fabric of who we are as professionals. Our legacy is not only our subordinate leaders and the leaders that they develop, but it is also the knowledge that we create together and the advancement of the profession itself.

The story of the Afghan Commander prep initiative (Chapter Ten) underscores what is possible when a profession has a third-generation mindset. Members of the profession came together in service to the leaders of 3rd Brigade Combat Team/25th ID(L). Six Afghan-experienced company commanders and two FRG leaders met face-to-face with the 3rd BCT leaders; the CC team provided seventy copies of the book *Taliban*; and forty-one company commanders shared their hard-earned knowledge to create the *Afghan Commander AAR Book*. As a result, leaders were better prepared—their learning curves shifted—and the profession advanced.

However, it is what the 3rd BCT leaders are doing now that reveals the longer term impact of this effort. The AAR book, for example, was so helpful that they created an even better one for their successors. It is guaranteed to help the next rotation of leaders—OEF VI—arrive better prepared than anyone who has gone before them. In the same way that the 3rd BCT commanders gained immeasurably from the original *Afghan Commander AAR Book*, they are now passing it on through the new *OEF V AAR Book*.

---

[2] Don M. Snider, Gayle Watkins and Lloyd Matthews (eds.), *The Future of the Army Profession,* 2002.

[3] This insight is drawn from our own experience and is supported by several scholars in the field of military professions: Andrew Abbott, 1988; Paul Christopher, 1995; Don M. Snider, Gayle Watkins and Lloyd Matthews, 2002.

Through the lens of third-generation leadership, the 3rd BCT leaders were inspired and equipped to do for others what had been done for them. And we can envision the leaders of OEF VI continuing to build upon this legacy and more effectively sharing their hard-won knowledge with the leaders of OEF VII.

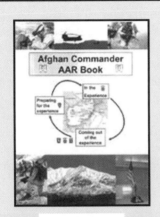

1st AAR Book

2nd AAR Book

Example from the *OEF V AAR Book:*

*Be sure your Soldiers are always ready to react to contact. During one particular operation, the company made multiple movements via helicopter. Soldiers became complacent after conducting several without incident. During the final movement, an aircraft sat down under ACM small arms and RPG assault. The element did not expect contact—they expected the norm, and the contact caught them off guard. Some individuals getting off the CH-47 did not know they were under fire until after the bird lifted off. Anytime, anywhere—the ACM forces can strike; your Soldiers must be prepared for it at all times. —**Chris Owen, B/2-5 IN, OEF 5***

Sharing Knowledge, Advancing the Profession

Dan Morgan has been a man on a mission to capture his learning and to share it with his comrades. Prior to taking command of HHC/3-502nd, Dan started journaling his experiences, an initiative that turned into the Commanders' Log section of CC.mil and inspired other commanders to do the same. Through his journal entries, we gained access to Dan's thinking and experiences—his change-of-command inventories, innovative training ideas, and the challenges of a company commander preparing for combat operations. During Operation Iraqi Freedom, Dan continued to journal and share what was working and what wasn't working. Dan's contribution was more than answers; it included access to the why behind his insights, which is the kind of thing that makes CC a developmental community. By engaging in the conversation—by being connected to Dan Morgan—successive generations of commanders develop their judgment and become more effective leaders.

Donn Hill has contributed to CC in many ways, to include submitting his training management SOP. The SOP has become a CC classic—and it shows how sharing even one great idea or tool can make a lasting impact on the profession. We could go on and on with testimonies about the impact that Donn had by sharing it, but the point is that Donn's simple act of submitting the SOP meant that thousands of leaders could benefit from his experience. Moreover, company commanders are building upon the SOP, creating an iterative process of learning and development.

By engaging in CC, leaders gain access to knowledge—however, more powerfully for the profession, they gain a platform to share their ideas, lessons learned, and wisdom born of experience. They are enabled to be professionals on a scale never before possible. Third-generation thinking, applied to professional forums, happens when you contribute to the forum with the insight that it is not just a place to get something or even to "give back," but as a place where the profession grows. We envision current company commanders investing in the next generation of commanders in the same way that past commanders are now investing in them. In doing so, we will develop together a leadership engine that will create future leaders long after we are gone.

Retiring warriors value the memories of victories won and challenges overcome, but on that day when they take their uniform off, their deepest meaning is found in the difference that they made—both in the lives of Soldiers and in the effectiveness of the profession. Their legacy is the leaders and the Army that they leave behind.

Project yourself forward and picture yourself standing in front of your family, friends, and comrades in arms at your own retirement ceremony. As you look back on your career, what stands out for you? Where do you find the most meaning?

"What will your legacy be?"

Appendix 1

Other Professional Forums

...*PlatoonLeader, FRG, S3-XO, S1net, and CAVNET*

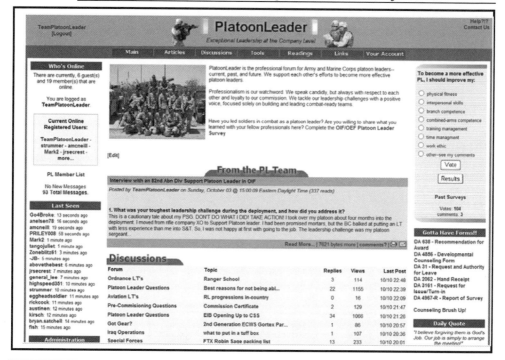

PL forum member feedback

"I want to thank the PL team for doing what you guys are doing. I am making it a personal quest to give out as much information about being over here as I can to my future peers—so if there is something else I can help with, please let me know. Thank you again." –John T. Soron, from Iraq

PlatoonLeader is present, future, and past platoon leaders. The forum exists to improve the effectiveness of Army platoon leaders.

The heart and soul of PlatoonLeader is current platoon leaders and their ongoing professional conversation. In this forum, platoon leaders across the globe connect in conversation about the things that matter most when it comes to leading Soldiers and building combat-ready teams.

A combat-leader interview on the PlatoonLeader forum

"One of my greatest leadership challenges was operating in an environment where planning and rehearsals were just about non-existent. More times than not, I was giving the OPORD to the squad leaders as the Soldiers were loading the trucks or prepping to leave the compound on foot. The squad leaders then were giving the plan to the soldiers *ON* the truck or enroute. Somehow, the Soldiers always got the mission done with very few kinks. Personally, I attribute that to having some of the best NCOs and Soldiers in the Army. Eventually, that just became the norm, so everyone knew what to do when they were given a general task." –LT J.M. Phillips

Connect at http://PlatoonLeader.army.mil

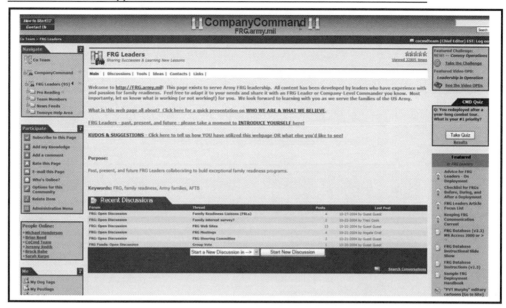

FRG leader forum member feedback

"I LOVE how every facet of FRG is covered—even things I didn't know to prepare for. I like being able to read the experiences of others so that I can then take the ideas shared and adapt them to my own situation. I love having the forms, checklists, etc available to me for adapting. It's a God-send!! I love this site!! THANK YOU!" –Kristina Holt

The FRG leader forum is present, past, and future FRG leadership collaborating to build exceptional family readiness programs. Ongoing conversations about Soldiers and families allow participants to share ideas, tools, and resources.

The forum exists to:

Connect present and future FRG leaders with experienced leaders who are passionate about FRG and have a desire to share with others.

Resource Army FRG Leadership with useful tools, tips, ideas, and information.

Serve Company-Level Leadership by working to build exceptional Family Readiness Groups.

A discussion post on the FRG leader forum

"One challenge I faced as an FRG leader was reaching out to the single Soldiers. The real winner was our 'Adopt a Soldier' program, which we started while the unit was deployed for a year. Each FRG member 'adopted' a Soldier, wrote him/her letters, and sent care packages on a regular basis. When we sent the information out via email, the response was overwhelming! We had sisters, mothers-in-law, etc. adopting single Soldiers—I believe we ended up with every single Soldier having at least two sponsors. The thanks and gratitude when they returned home was truly heart-felt and sincere!" –Melissa from Germany

Connect at http://FRG.army.mil

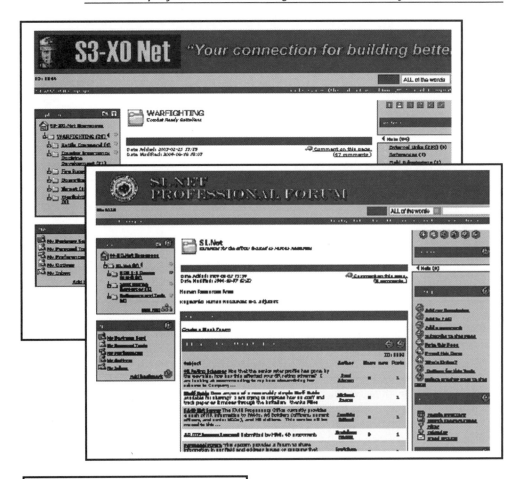

A new S3 is able to tap into cutting-edge ideas on the best ways to train his battalion for convoy operations in Iraq.

*****

An experienced XO is able to pass on her hard-earned lessons about making the maintenance system work in the harsh and barren environment of Afghanistan.

*****

An S1 on the ground in Iraq is able to get real-time input on casualty operations from a peer S1 in theatre.

S3-XOnet and S1net are present, past, and future Operations/ Executive Officers and Unit S1s. These forums exist to improve the effectiveness of staff officers who are serving leaders at the tip of the spear. Through these professional forums, leaders share lessons learned, MOIs, SOPs, and many other essential tools of the staff officer trade.

Connect at https://S3-XOnet.army.mil
https://S1net.army.mil

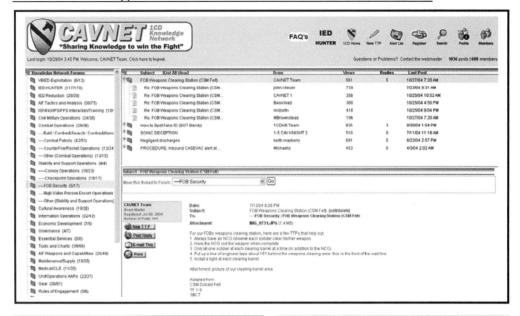

Combat in many ways is a learning race. The opponent who is able to learn, adapt, and share that learning most rapidly will have an advantage. With this in mind, S.L.A. Marshall, in his book *Men Against Fire,* captures why a forum like CAVNET is so critical to combat effectiveness: "During war, it oftentimes happens that one company, by trial and error, finds the true solution for some acute problem which concerns everyone.… A good company idea in tactics is likely to remain confined to one company indefinitely, even though it would be of benefit to the whole military establishment." –S.L.A. Marshall

CAVNET exists to improve the effectiveness of First Cavalry Division company-level leaders and units engaged in combat operations in Iraq.

It is a user-driven forum designed to horizontally distribute emerging tactics, techniques, and procedures being developed by company-level leaders. Through this classified forum, leaders in combat are able to share ideas, tools, and lessons born out of experience with their comrades—foxhole to foxhole.

On 16 June 2004—in response to a 1st Cav company-level unit experience—a posting flashed across CAVNET warning of Anti Iraqi Forces booby-trapping posters of Muqtada Al Sadr. The enemy had identified the US procedure of tearing down propaganda posters and developed a method to booby-trap the signs with an improvised explosive device (IED). A company commander in another sector read the post and then informed his Soldiers of the emerging enemy tactic, warning them to "be on the lookout" for suspicious signs. Within days, a patrol from this company discovered a propaganda sign. Rather than just ripping down the sign, they took precautions and found that it *was* booby-trapped with an IED!

CAVNET was established by MG Pete Chiarelli (1st Cavalry Division commander). This ground-breaking forum has been led by Major Patrick Michaelis.

Appendix 2

From Our Bookshelf

...Books that made a difference for us

Reading books—especially in the fields of leadership, learning, and organizational effectiveness—has been an essential part of our experience. The conversations that they have sparked and the insights that we have gained are embedded in the way that we think and work. The books we recommend here are representative of the many that have impacted us in our work with the CompanyCommand professional forum.

We need to prepare ourselves for the possibility that sometimes **big changes** follow from small events, and that sometimes these changes can happen very quickly.
-*The Tipping Point* (Gladwell)

Those who turn good into **great** are motivated by a deep **creative** urge and an inner compulsion for sheer unadulterated **excellence** for its own sake. Those who build and perpetuate mediocrity, in contrast, are motivated more by the fear of being left behind.
-*Good to Great* (Collins)

Successful, long-lasting communities almost always start off small, simple and focused, and then **grow organically over time**—adding breadth, depth and complexity in response to the changing needs of the members, and the changing conditions of the environment.
-*Building Community on the Web* (Kim)

A community of practice is not just a web site, a database, or a collection of best practices. It is a group of people who interact, learn together, build relationships, and in the process develop a sense of belonging and mutual commitment.
-*Cultivating Communities of Practice* (Wenger, McDermott, Snyder)

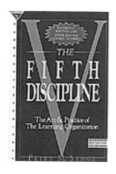

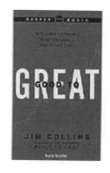

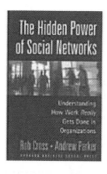

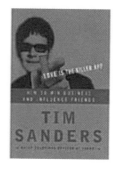

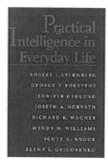

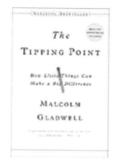

The Art of Possibility: Transforming Professional and Personal Life Rosamund Stone Zander and Benjamin Zander (2000)	*The Cluetrain Manifesto: The End of Business As Usual* Rick Levine, Christopher Locke, Doc Searls, and David Weinberger (2000)	*Common Knowledge: How Companies Thrive by Sharing What They Know* Nancy M. Dixon (2000)	*Community Building On The Web: Secret Strategies for Successful Online Communities* Amy Jo Kim (2000)
Cultivating Communities of Practice: A Guide to Managing Knowledge Etienne Wenger, Richard McDermott, and William M. Snyder (2002)	*The Fifth Discipline: The Art & Practice of The Learning Organization* Peter M. Senge (1990)	*The Future of the Army Profession* Don M. Snider, Gayle Watkins, and Lloyd Matthews (eds.) (2002) Note: 2nd edition is forthcoming.	*Good to Great: Why Some Companies Make the Leap...and Others Don't* Jim Collins (2001)
The Hidden Power of Social Networks: Understanding How Work Really Gets Done in Organizations Rob Cross and Andrew Parker (2004)	*The Leadership Challenge, 3rd Ed.* Jim Kouzes and Barry Posner (2002)	*Leveraging Communities of Practice for Strategic Advantage* Hubert Saint-Onge and Debra Wallace (2003)	*Love is the Killer App: How to Win Business and Influence Friends* Tim Sanders (2002)
Practical Intelligence in Everyday Life Robert J. Sternberg, George B. Forsythe, et al. (2000)	*The Social Life of Information* John Seely Brown and Paul Duguid (2000)	*Taking the Guidon: Exceptional Leadership at the Company Level* Nate Allen and Tony Burgess (2001)	*The Tipping Point: How Little Things Can Make a Big Difference* Malcolm Gladwell (2000)

Acknowledgements

First, we want to thank the CC team—the leaders who do the work of the CompanyCommand professional forum, often behind the scenes. Without them, there would be no CompanyCommand forum and, therefore, no book. In addition to their work serving company commanders, many team members subjected themselves to our interviews and never-ending barrages of questions, and—if that wasn't enough—they read our work and gave us much-needed feedback. Thank you!

Writing a book is never the work of the authors alone, and that is true to the extreme with this book. It is with great joy that we thank the amazing people that have so directly supported us in the creation of this book:

The Army CIO/G6 team that supported this book-writing project—especially Lieutenant General Boutelle, Mr. Winkler, Lieutenant Colonel Harris, Laura Petrosian, and Rick Morris. We greatly appreciate the work they did to make this project a reality.

Loren Gary and Lisa Maria Noudehou, who spent countless hours editing and proofreading the book at different stages in the writing process. The quality of this book is a reflection of their competence and eye for detail.

Colonel Forsythe saw the potential in the CompanyCommand and PlatoonLeader forums and championed the cause. We are forever indebted to him for the faith he placed in us, the support he has infused into the movement, and for his continued mentorship.

Lieutenant General Lennox and Brigadier General Kaufman also recognized the impact that professional forums could have on the Army and stepped up to the plate to make sure that we could continue growing the idea.

The West Point support team has been amazing, and we would like to acknowledge the efforts of Jan Jordal, Laura Maxwell, Bobbie Ryan, Cheryl Rau, Tim Wright, Colonel Preczewski, Colonel Klinefelter, Lieutenant Colonel Buchanan, Lieutenant Colonel Carver, Lieutenant Colonel Dalton, Deb Scully, John Blanc, Millie Jones, Barbara Walker, Chris Lilly, Pat Campbell, Lesley Beckstrom, and Sergeant First Class Creamer.

General Gordon R. Sullivan has been a source of inspiration and encouragement ever since he came across CompanyCommand in 2001 and immediately wrote to offer his support. It is an honor and a privilege to have his words on the back cover of this book.

Etienne Wenger, Kent Greenes, and Hubert Saint-Onge for making time to share their vast knowledge. They are true mentors.

Michelle Magnus did an amazing job of illustrating Etienne, Kent, and Hubert for Chapter Eleven. Her work helps create the sense that the three mentors really are there with you as you read.

The incredible Great Impressions team—especially Vickie Goble, Marcos Felan, and Cathy Brignole. Their competence and passion for excellence is inspiring.

Jody Harmon (armorart.com), who enthusiastically responded to our late request for help designing the cover. Jody has illustrated *Armor Magazine* for sixteen years, and we count it a privilege to have his work on the cover.

Steve Salva and the team at Groove Networks (www.groove.net). We used *Groove Virtual Office* as a collaborative writing tool throughout the book-writing process—it would be hard to imagine writing the book without it.

The team at Tomoye, Inc.—our technology platform provider—has been an exceptional partner. Their vision and desire to deliver world-class value makes working together a privilege. Many aspects of our Web site design are possible because of what the Tomoye team has done.

Our academic advisors in our respective graduate programs at The George Washington and Penn State Universities, whose input and understanding for the time this book required was priceless: Ted Rosen, Chris Kayes, Bill Halal, Phyllis Langton, Michael Stankosky, Francesco Calabrese, William Schulte, Chris Hoadley, and Jack Carroll.

The good people at Felicita, PA, who took care of us while we gathered to strategize and do much of the book writing.

Finally, and as you might guess, most importantly to us—we would like to thank our families for their unbelievable support during this book-writing experience. We specifically thank Joan, Ashley, Kristi, Ryan, Barbara, TJ, Jessie, Jake, Cathy, Aaron, Sean, Kyle, Luke, Wendy, Nathan, and Emma. Without your love and understanding, this book just would not have happened.

Index